Devotions for Deconstructors, Disciples, and Doubters

DEVOTIONS FOR DECONSTRUCTORS, DISCIPLES, AND DOUBTERS

Dr. Jason Lee McKinney

WordCrafts Press

Contents

1

Desperate Enough for Healing to Act in Faith

A man in the crowd answered. "Teacher," he said, "I brought you my son. He is controlled by an evil spirit. Because of this, my son can't speak anymore. When the spirit takes hold of him, it throws him to the ground. He foams at the mouth. He grinds his teeth. And his body becomes stiff. I asked your disciples to drive out the spirit. But they couldn't do it."

"You unbelieving people!" Jesus replied. "How long do I have to stay with you? How long do I have to put up with you? Bring the boy to me."

So they brought him. As soon as the spirit saw Jesus, it threw the boy into a fit. He fell to the ground. He rolled around and foamed at the mouth.

Jesus asked the boy's father, "How long has he been like this?"

"Since he was a child," he answered. "The spirit has often thrown him into fire or water to kill him. But if you can do anything, take pity on us. Please help us."

"If you can'?" said Jesus. "Everything is possible for the one who believes."

Right away the boy's father cried out, "I do believe! Help me overcome my unbelief!"

Jesus saw that a crowd was running over to see what was

happening. Then he ordered the evil spirit to leave the boy. "You spirit that makes him unable to hear and speak!" he said. "I command you, come out of him. Never enter him again."

The spirit screamed. It shook the boy wildly. Then it came out of him. The boy looked so lifeless that many people said, "He's dead." But Jesus took him by the hand. He lifted the boy to his feet, and the boy stood up.

~Mark 9:17–27 NIVR

"'Lord, I believe; help my unbelief'... is the most natural and most human and most agonizing prayer in the gospels, and I think it is the foundation prayer of faith."

~Flannery O'Connor

"Do not waste time bothering whether you *love* your neighbor; act as if you did. As soon as we do this we find one of the great secrets. When you are behaving as if you loved someone, you will presently come to love him."

~C. S. Lewis

O'Connor described the famous prayer in this passage as the most human. I think this is in no small part because it wreaks of desperation. We humans are often desperate. Doubt and desperation pair together like wine and cheese (or peanut butter and jelly if you are Baptist). It is what we do with our doubt that matters. In a very real way, the father in this passage is acting out his faith despite his doubt because of this desperation. To paraphrase C.S. Lewis, the father wasn't bothered by whether he had faith in Jesus, he was going to act as if he did, and he found the great secret, by bringing his son to Jesus, by acting as though he had the faith and by calling on Jesus to help him have more faith, he discovered all the faith he needed.

Imagine that morning, the father woke up extra early having

heard there was a teacher and his disciples in town who could possibly, potentially, maybe heal his son who had been sick, tortured by demons for a long time. The father had probably heard these promises of healing many times over. He would likely be fighting the inner skeptic in his mind. Vacillating between getting his son up and making the trip and dismissing this rumor of healing as a bunch of fools believing in fairytales. Yet this father did decide to give it one more try.

The father got his son out of bed, dressed him, made breakfast, and then transported his son to this teacher. We can imagine bringing the son to the crowded area would cause a lot of stress and anxiety in the father given that his son could go into convulsions and fits at any moment. We can also imagine that this family's situation was not unknown to much of the crowd. As the father weaved his way through the crowd, already stressed by the potential of one of his son's episodes, he would have heard the murmurs and whispers about his son's condition. Not for the first time but for the thousandth time. Hearing the crowd say, "can you believe he brought him here?" "This is an embarrassment to the whole town."

Yet this father guided his son through the crowd and with every "pardon me, excuse me" made his way to Jesus. Once the father got within ear shot of the disciples, he had to be vulnerable enough to tell complete strangers about his son's condition and ask them to heal him. The disciples tried but failed to heal his son like countless doctors, priests, and healers' before them. Yet this father did not stop. He made his way through more of the crowd to Jesus. He had to take a deep breath and announce his family's struggle, embarrassment, issues—basically he had to publicly air his family's dirty laundry to someone he did not know. Then the worst happened, his son went into a fit right in front of everyone. Right in front of this teacher. The father humbled himself and asked this teacher to take pity on him and his son. The father wasn't sure this would help. He didn't know if healing was possible.

Jesus told him, "Everything is possible for the one who believes."

Jesus was asking this man to believe against all odds, believe against all the past hurts and failures to bring about relief for his son. Verse 24 states the boys father right away affirms his faith and cries out for help. As an even bigger crowd of rubber-neckers was running over to see his boy convulse and foam at the mouth, Jesus healed the boy.

We often read this father's prayer as a feeble half-hearted attempt at faith, but it is far from that. It is the climax to every act of faith that led to that declaration. Every step of the way to that prayer this father acted in faith. Each sandal he put on, each step, every ignored comment was an act of faith. Yes, he was a desperate man who wanted healing for his son, and this drove him. His desperation for healing drove him to overcome the hurt from past failed attempts at healing his son, his own skepticism, the crowd's jeers, his pride or even self-respect and act out faith. This father was believing in every moment right up to his crying, "I do believe! Help me overcome my unbelief!"

Despite our doubts are we desperate enough for healing to act in faith until we receive the answers? Are we desperate enough to act in faith even if we don't get the answers? The father had no idea whether Jesus would physically heal his son, and yet he acted in faith. We should do the same.

Father in heaven I believe! Help my unbelief. Help me be so desperate to find you that I am willing to behave as if you are there even when I am not sure you are. Jesus, Teacher, I seek the healing that only you can bring. Holy Spirit help me fight my own skeptic nature and keep searching for you and trusting you will bring the answers. In Jesus name. Amen.

2

Doubt Is Not Dismissal

Thomas was one of the twelve disciples. He was also called Didymus. He was not with the other disciples when Jesus came. So they told him, "We have seen the Lord!"

But he said to them, "First I must see the nail marks in his hands. I must put my finger where the nails were. I must put my hand into his side. Only then will I believe."

A week later, Jesus' disciples were in the house again. Thomas was with them. Even though the doors were locked, Jesus came in and stood among them. He said, "May peace be with you!"

Then he said to Thomas, "Put your finger here. See my hands. Reach out your hand and put it into my side. Stop doubting and believe."

Thomas said to him, "My Lord and my God!"

Then Jesus told him, "Because you have seen me, you have believed. Blessed are those who have not seen me but still have believed."

~John 20:24–29 NIVR

"The weakest believer is a child of God, and true faith, though at first like a grain of mustard seed, is interested in all the promises of the gospel. If it be true, it will grow; it

5

will attain to a more simple dependence upon its great object and will work its way through a thousand doubts and fears (which, for a season, are not without their use) till at length the weak Christian becomes strong in faith, strong in the Lord, and is enabled to say, "I know whom I have believed."
~John Newton

"If Jesus is the model of perfect faith, and his twin is Thomas, who models doubt, then what we understand is that faith and doubt are not antitheses—they're twins."
~Mark Schaefer

This is perhaps the most famous passage about doubt in the scripture. So much so that the phrase "doubting Thomas" is synonymous with someone who must see it to believe it. On the one hand it is hard to fathom how Thomas could be hesitant about Jesus' ability to rise from the dead. He had been with Jesus when Jesus raised Lazarus already (John 11:38–44); had seen Jesus raise the widow's son from the dead (Luke 7:11–17); and though he was not permitted inside the house, he was privy to the eyewitness accounts of Jairus' daughter being dead and then surely saw her alive with his own eyes (Luke 8:40–42). Thomas was there when Jesus raised three people from the dead. How could he doubt Jesus' ability to raise himself from the dead? For some of us skepticism comes easy, and faith comes hard.

Thomas was doubting, but he did not take a posture of dismissal. Thomas asked for evidence. Was Thomas doubting Jesus' ability to rise from the dead, or was he just doubting his friends' testimony? Most likely it was some of both. But Thomas was not refusing to believe at all. In fact, he says first he must see then he would believe. Thomas was questioning the other disciples' testimony about the risen Christ, but he was not refusing to believe them. Thomas needed more evidence.

For seven days Thomas lived in this doubt without the evidence he was asking for, then Jesus showed up literally in the flesh. Thomas was able to see and touch Jesus, and Thomas responded with faith saying, "My Lord and my God!"

Jesus responds by saying Thomas received the physical evidence of the risen Christ and therefore believed, but it would have been better if Thomas believed without the evidence. If Thomas believed Jesus could raise himself from the dead and if Thomas would have believed what his friends were telling him, it would have been better. Friends, this should not discourage us but encourage us. None of us had access to the direct experiential evidence Thomas had before he doubted the resurrection. We were not with Jesus at any of his teachings, we weren't there to experience any of his miracles. We only have the testimony and accounts of Thomas and his friends and yet we have believed. Sure, some of us require more evidence than others, but all of us believe without seeing and touching the resurrected Christ. For those of us who require more evidence, Jesus is there to give it just like he did Thomas if we can keep our doubt from slipping in dismissal.

Father in Heaven, I see so much of myself in Thomas. I also see how you treated Thomas. Help me to find comfort in the grace you showed Thomas. When I am doubting you or your people and needing more evidence, help me to remember that you offered evidence and comfort to Thomas. Help me to be confident that you will offer me the same. May I never dismiss you but always trust the evidence is coming. In Jesus name. Amen.

3

But Jesus Said Not To Doubt

Early in the morning, Jesus was on his way back to Jerusalem. He was hungry. He saw a fig tree by the road. He went up to it but found nothing on it except leaves. Then he said to it, "May you never bear fruit again!" Right away the tree dried up. When the disciples saw this, they were amazed. "How did the fig tree dry up so quickly?" they asked.

Jesus replied, "What I'm about to tell you is true. You must have faith and not doubt. Then you can do what was done to the fig tree. And you can say to this mountain, 'Go and throw yourself into the sea.' It will be done. If you believe, you will receive what you ask for when you pray."

~Matthew 21:18–22 NIVR

"Doubt arises within the context of faith. It is a wistful longing to be sure of the things in which we trusted. But it is not and need not be a problem."

~Alister McGrath

"Doubt is but another element of faith."

~Saint Augustine.

First off, in this passage, is it just me or does Jesus seem not hungry but hangry? I mean I am sure not to the point of sin, but he sure seems frustrated that tree didn't have any fruit for him to eat given that it already had leaves on it. Jesus being fully human was subject to all the natural laws the rest of us are. Humans get hungry and need to eat. Jesus had to eat, sleep, use the restroom just like the rest of us. Jesus wanted to eat some fig and there was none on the tree he found. Jesus, perhaps frustrated or perhaps just to teach the disciples a lesson (or maybe a bit of both literal and symbolic), told the fig tree it would not produce fruit again and caused the tree to dry up right there. It is interesting that Jesus was hungry because of the laws of nature but choose to transcend the laws of nature to dry the tree up and thus not satisfy his hunger. Jesus could have just as easily caused the tree to instantly grow figs as he caused it to dry up. This fact leads me to conclude Jesus chose to dry up the tree to teach the disciples something. But teach them what? Well, what else but about faith. The tree had the appearance of fruit but actual bore no fruit. Actual authentic faith produces fruit.

In verse 22 Jesus is using obvious hyperbole which was a common way to teach in ancient Israel. Christians' ability to cast a mountain into the sea is not meant to be taken literally. The mountain is symbolic of something impossible. We still today use this literary device all the time, I mean Jesus was as hungry as a horse and dying of starvation, and he had already told the disciples a million times to have faith (see what I did there). However, Jesus just performed a metaphysical, beyond nature, literally supernatural feat by instantly drying up a fig tree. So, while using hyperbole of something that is impossible to make a point, Jesus is not dismissing the supernatural either. Jesus said his followers in John 14:12 would do greater things than he, and that included things that are beyond nature.

Doubt is the attitude of equally questioning all paradigms,

information, rules, presuppositions, and all other points that govern one's understanding of the world. Remember faith and doubt are not in opposition. Jesus just got through making the point that faith produces fruit. To have a worldview (and we all do) we must operate with the assumptions that certain things are real and true. We must operate with faith to produce fruit even as it co-exists with doubt. Jesus is asking the disciples to give deference to their faith and not their doubt. Many of these guys will doubt again and again, and yet they are the same guys who changed the world. Jesus is not unaware of that future. The disciples had just witnessed something that was beyond nature; Jesus was asking them to trust what they had just witnessed and operate on it. Faith does not produce fruit because it does not share head or heart space with doubt. Faith produces fruit when we believe what Jesus demonstrates to us despite doubt. Which one are we going to give the most weight—faith or doubt? Every time we pray, we are operating in faith and giving it priority over our doubt. This is the faith Jesus is speaking about. Every time we pray there is a "act as if"-ness that is having faith and not doubt. This is what can move mountains and dry up fig trees. Even if we are hangry.

Father, Help me! Help me have the faith to have faith through my doubt. Lord give me a true faith that produces fruit and not just leaves. Holy Spirit help me to act as if the impossible is possible and difficult is bearable until you give me the belief to believe it and the evidence to build me up in the faith. In the name of Jesus, Amen.

4

John the Baptist was in prison. When he heard about the actions of the Messiah, he sent his disciples to him. They asked Jesus, "Are you the one who is supposed to come? Or should we look for someone else?" Jesus replied, "Go back to John. Report to him what you hear and see. Blind people receive sight. Disabled people walk. Those who have skin diseases are made 'clean.' Deaf people hear. Those who are dead are raised to life. And the good news is preached to those who are poor. Blessed is anyone who does not give up their faith because of me."

As John's disciples were leaving, Jesus began to speak to the crowd about John. He said, "What did you go out into the desert to see? Tall grass waving in the wind? If not, what did you go out to see? A man dressed in fine clothes? No. People who wear fine clothes are in kings' palaces. Then what did you go out to see? A prophet? Yes, I tell you, and more than a prophet. He is the one written about in Scripture. It says,

'I will send my messenger ahead of you.
He will prepare your way for you.' (Malachi 3:1)
                                            ~Matthew 11:2–10 NIVR

"I do not believe there ever existed a Christian yet, who

11

did not now and then doubt his interest in Jesus. I think, when a man says, "I never doubt," it is quite time for us to doubt him."

~Charles Spurgeon

"Be patient toward all that is unsolved in your heart and try to love the questions themselves, like locked rooms and like books that are now written in a very foreign tongue. Do not now seek the answers, which cannot be given you because you would not be able to live them. And the point is, to live everything. Live the questions now. Perhaps you will then gradually, without noticing it, live along some distant day into the answer."

~Rainer Maria Rilke

Friends we all doubt now and then. Most of us doubt our faith more than occasionally, and some of us (like me) walk with the permanent limp of doubt. It is a part of our daily lives, and that is okay. I love Matthew 11:2–10 for a couple of reasons: 1) who it is that is doing the doubting and 2) how Jesus reacts to the doubt. John the Baptist was raised in church, he was a preacher's kid, a prophet, and as a prophet he was a vocational Christian. John was the very one who first recognized and announced Jesus as Messiah. In fact, it was John who baptized Jesus. If anyone wasn't supposed to doubt, if anyone shouldn't doubt, it was John, and yet when John was in prison facing his own death, he did in fact doubt. What John did with his doubt was key. He didn't deny or hide his doubt (v.2), but rather he leaned into his faith. He asked the big questions, and he trusted Jesus to respond (v.2). In essence John was saying the same thing as the father desperate to see his boy healed in Mark 9:24, "I believe. Help my unbelief."

Jesus did respond but not as you might expect. Jesus did not respond by telling John he should know better, or that of all people he expected better of him, or that "you just got to have faith brother." No. Jesus didn't condemn John for doubting like doubt is the opposite of faith. No, Jesus reassured John (v.4–6) treating doubt as a natural part of faith. Jesus didn't ask John to "just believe" but rather Jesus gave evidence of his supernatural divinity (healing, miracles) that could be and were perceived through the senses (the very senses Jesus healed—they saw the blind regain sight and heard the deaf able to hear again). Then Jesus went a step further. Jesus did not chastise John for doubting but rather he defended and honored John to the crowds (v.7–10).

Friends it should be a comfort that we all doubt from time to time, and Jesus is not shocked, put off, or offended by that doubt. As Jude 1:22 challenges us to do, Jesus is merciful to doubters. Jesus defends and honors us for having the faith to come to him with our doubts.

Father in heaven, thank you for not being put off or offended by my doubt. Thank you for your patience and kindness toward me. Jesus help me to let go of my need for certainty and embrace true faith. Lord, you did not condemn John for doubting; help me to believe you, don't condemn me now for having doubt. In Jesus name. Amen.

5

The Heartbeat of the Savior

After he had said this, Jesus' spirit was troubled. He said, "What I'm about to tell you is true. One of you is going to hand me over to my enemies." His disciples stared at one another. They had no idea which one of them he meant. The disciple Jesus loved was next to him at the table. Simon Peter motioned to that disciple. He said, "Ask Jesus which one he means."

The disciple was leaning back against Jesus. He asked him, "Lord, who is it?"

~John 13:21–25 NIVR

"You will trust God to the degree you know you are loved by Him."

~Brennan Manning

"For those united to him, the heart of Jesus is not a rental; it is your new permanent residence. You are not a tenant; you are a child. His heart is not a ticking time bomb; his heart is the green pastures and still waters of endless reassurances of his presence and comfort, whatever our present spiritual accomplishments. It is who he is."

~Dane Ortlund

14

As a very young child I remember often waking up in my bed and hearing the faint sounds of the TV and seeing the light shadows bounce off my bedroom ceiling late at night. I would grab my blanket and groggily make my way to the living room where I would find my dad (all 6' 5" 250 lbs of him) lying flat on his back watching Rasslin' (not wrestling but Rasslin'). Without a word I would lay on his chest. I could feel the strength of his muscular chest (my dad was quite the athlete), and placing my ear on it I could hear his heartbeat in steady rhythm. I was gently rocked like a boat on the ocean by the air filling and exhaling from his lungs. I felt completely and utterly safe. I would drift in and out of sleep. In the times of wake, I would ask him questions. Sometimes about rasslin' and sometimes about life. I had no fear that he would reject my questions no matter how simple or complex they were. I knew my father had me and wasn't too troubled to give an answer even when my young mind could not yet understand the answer he was giving. I would raise my head off his chest, ask my question, and then put my ear back on his chest to await his answer. When the answer came, I could not only hear his voice in the room through the air but also hear it resonate in his chest. The cadence of his words mixed with the rhythm of his heartbeat and the ebb and flow of his breath to become hymn like. I had no fear or shame in asking my questions, I simply asked and then laid my head back on his chest.

John 13:21–25 details that famous and final Passover meal near the end of Jesus' public ministry where Jesus announces he will be betrayed by one of the twelve. As readers we often look at the betrayal and even imagine the panic of the disciples trying to figure out which one was the betrayer, and we miss the interaction of Jesus and John. The custom of the time when eating meals was to lie with the left arm supported on a cushion, and the feet stretched out behind, so that the right hand remained free for eating. John was sitting to the right of Jesus (indicating a closeness between the two). John refers to himself as the one Jesus loved.

In verse 22 it says the disciples where at a loss for which one would betray Jesus. In verse 23 it says that Peter wanted John to get the answer for them. Why didn't Peter ask Jesus himself? Peter after all was the leader. Was it just because John was closer in proximity or was it because John was *closer*? Was it because John trusted Jesus more. John described himself as one who was loved by Jesus, he had a comfort and a closeness with Jesus that was different. Perhaps Peter knew John was comfortable asking Jesus hard questions. We can almost picture John leaning back with the crown of his head on the chest of his best friend, his mentor, his teacher, the savior, God himself. Looking up to make eye contact and almost whispering, "Lord, who is it?" When John leaned back on Jesus' chest he could hear the heartbeat of the savior, he could feel the breath of life going in and out of his lungs. In that safety and intimacy John simply asked Jesus his question. That same savior is inviting us in our troubles and confusion to lean back against his chest, hear his heartbeat and feel his breath and simply ask our questions. All we need to do is keep our head on his chest and listen for the cadence of his words mixed with the rhythm of his heartbeat and the ebb and flow of his breath. We should feel no fear or shame in asking our questions. Jesus has us. All we have to do is raise our head off his chest, ask our question, and then put our ear back on his chest to await his answer.

Father in Heaven, whether I am the one who has been betrayed or I am the betrayer, don't let me go. Pull me to your chest. Let me hear your heartbeat and feel your breath. May it bring comfort and confidence that I can ask my questions of you, cry on your chest if I need to, and you won't reject me. Nothing I have done or has been done to me will change who and what I am to you. I am the one Jesus loves. In Jesus name. Amen.

6

You've Got the Wrong Person

Moses spoke to the Lord. He said, "Lord, I've never been a good speaker. And I haven't gotten any better since you spoke to me. I don't speak very well at all."

The Lord said to him, "Who makes human beings able to talk? Who makes them unable to hear or speak? Who makes them able to see? Who makes them blind? It is I, the Lord. Now go. I will help you speak. I will teach you what to say." But Moses said, "Lord, please send someone else to do it." Then the Lord became very angry with Moses. He said, "What about your brother, Aaron the Levite? I know he can speak well. He is already on his way to meet you. He will be glad to see you. Speak to him. Tell him what to say. I will help both of you speak. I will teach you what to do. He will speak to the people for you. He will be like your mouth. And you will be like God to him. But take this walking stick in your hand. You will be able to do signs with it."

~Exodus 4:10–17 NIVR

"Faith is taking the first step even when you don't see the whole staircase."

~Martin Luther King, Jr.

"Pharaoh had more reason to be afraid of stammering Moses than of the most fluent talker in Egypt…if the Lord be with us in our natural weakness, we shall be girded with supernatural power."

~Charles Spurgeon

Doubt comes in two primary categories—global doubt and local doubt. Global doubt is to doubt everything while local doubt is to doubt a particular experience or a particular set of information. Global Doubt is doubting the existence of God or existence itself, while local doubts are those are doubts about a particular sense experience or some other occurrence at a particular point in time or, in the case of Moses, doubting his ability to do what he was being called to do. Moses was not doubting God's existence in this passage; Moses was literally speaking to God in a burning bush. What Moses was doubting was his own ability and by proxy God's wisdom.

Moses had a speech impediment, so he was fearful of speaking to both his own people and to Pharaoh. Moses was so afraid that he pushed back to God telling God basically he had the wrong person for the job. God reassured him, gave him signs, and yet Moses still protested until God became angry and consented to let Moses' brother Aaron do the talking. But God did not remove the mission from Moses. Moses was to be the one to lead the Israelites out of Egypt. In Moses' protest to God, he reveals one of the reasons why God may have chosen him. Moses was modest and humble and knew he needed God. Sometimes our doubts are not a sign of weakness or a lack of faith but rather our doubts are meekness revealing itself. The rest of the story is that Moses did go, he did obey God, and he did lead the people out of Egypt. "So, Moses got his wife and sons. He put them on a donkey. Together they started back to Egypt." He doubted himself, he doubted God's wisdom in choosing him, but he went anyway, and he completed the mission. He took the first step. This should encourage us all to do the same even when we think God has got the wrong person for the job. When we doubt God's wisdom or our own abilities to complete a mission that God is calling us to, perhaps we are revealing the very reason God is being wise in his choosing of us. If we trust him, he will provide all the help we need.

> *Father in Heaven, like Moses I know I need you. I am aware that I am not aware of how much and how deep that need is, but I do know I need you. Help me to need you more. Lord there are places and circumstances in my life that don't make sense. Help me to trust your wisdom when a situation makes me doubt myself or you, when it is painful, confusing, embarrassing, frustrating, or fragile. In these moments may I act in faith even as doubt rages within me. In Jesus name. Amen.*

7

Suppose the Lord had not helped me.
Then I would soon have been lying quietly in the grave.
I said, "My foot is slipping."
But Lord, your faithful love kept me from falling.
I was very worried.
But your comfort brought me joy.
                              ~Psalm 94:17–19 NIVR

"Surely… we cannot imagine any certainty that is not tinged with doubt, or any assurance that is not assailed by some anxiety."

                              ~John Calvin

"Faith is holding on to uncertainties with passionate conviction."

                              ~Soren Kierkegaard

Doubt and anxiety are so synonymous in many of our experiences that we have a hard time even differentiating them. Anxiety is being apprehensive about the future. It is literally fear of the future. Therefore, if we are doubting what we believe about metaphysical and transcendent reality i.e. eternity which is the future then it makes sense why most doubters are also filled with anxiety. The question of whether there is a God is the biggest question there is. Tied to this is whether our lives have intrinsic meaning and how then are we to respond to God if God exists. The "I don't know" state we can find ourselves in through doubt directly impacts our view of the future. We can become overwhelmed by the temporal things we place too high a meaning on (if you find yourself here go read Ecclesiastes; it will soothe your soul) but then to add existential doubt on top of it is exhausting and mind bending.

Often when we are in a crisis of anxiety, we don't feel like God is helping. We can't sense how God is there at all. I have seasonal depression, and when I am in the middle of it, my inner imposter's messages of shame and dysfunction drown out any sense of God. I can get to the point where I feel like I am in a spiritual and emotional grave. It is in these times I must look backwards to the past to ward off the fears of the future. I need to remember the Lord's faithful love. Like the nation of Israel did in Joshua 4 or Moses did on Mount Sinai, we need to build altars of remembrance of the Lord's faithfulness in walking us through past worries or doubts to get us through our current worries and doubts. If the God we serve is who He says He is (and I believe He is) He will be faithful.

Father in Heaven, help me make the leap of faith I need to remember your faithfulness when the darkness of anxiety and doubt overtakes me. Jesus when I take assurance in you and anxiety tries to rob it from me lead not to stay in the cycle of anxiety but to search your words for more assurance. Holy Spirit you are the great comforter, be my comforter now. In Jesus name. Amen.

Part 1

8

Creativity from the Start

In the beginning God created the heavens and the earth.
~Genesis 1:1 NIVR

"Now everything that comes to be must of necessity come to be by the agency of some cause, for it is impossible for anything to come to be without cause."
~Plato, speaking from the character Timaeus of Locri

"A Christian, who realizes he has been made in the image of the Creator God and is therefore meant to be creative on a finite level, should certainly have more understanding of his responsibility to treat God's creation with sensitivity and should develop his talents to do something to beautify his little spot on the earth's surface."
~Edith Schaeffer

The Kalam cosmological argument re-popularized by William Lane Craig states:

1. Everything that begins to exist has a cause.
2. The universe began to exist.

3. Therefore, the universe has a cause.

When I sit down to write a song, I already have the idea of how the song will sound when I complete it. I hear the song as it will be before I begin. I can hear it produced in its entirety in my head. Now, does the song exist before I write it down or record it? (Well that depends on if you ask Plato or William Lane Craig.) Before I write the song, it exists as an idea. It is pure potential; once I write the song it is actualized. It then exists. But for the song to begin requires that I move it from idea into reality. I must, by my will, act for the song to exist. The point is songs have a beginning, and that beginning requires an act of creative will. Existence itself required an act of creative will to begin. Both science and religion agree the universe is not steady and did not always exist. There was a "time" when both time and the universe were not (1 Corinthians 2:7) Just like there was a time before your dad gave your mom that look, and things went down that you did not exist. You may have been an idea in your parent's mind before you existed or put more colloquially you were a gleam in your daddy's eye before you existed. The songs I write however do not have to exist; they only exist because I will them to exist by my creative action. The cause of the songs I write are me, the cause of you is Barry White or Silk Sonic music playing on your parents' romantic playlist and then your parents.

The universe had a beginning, and that beginning was a creative endeavor that was created from nothing. When I write a song, I am being creative in a sense, but I am not making up new chords or new notes for new melodies. In western music there are only twelve notes. I am not choosing any truly unique combination of those notes (and neither is anyone else). What I am doing is fashioning and combining different influences in the hopes of innovating something that gives the impression of being fresh or new. Humans are creative in a reflective way, but we are incapable of creating in a vacuum. We do not create anything from nothing. But in the case of the universe, which had to be created from nothing, the songwriter had to exist "before" the song could come into being. There are no songs without a songwriter. The difference is most songwriters are pulling from influences (music that inspires and language), but the universe was created from nothing. Friends only God can create from nothing, and it would take an almighty, all-powerful, and all-loving God to transform nothing into the universe as we know it (what little of it we know). Friends we should find, *In the beginning God created from nothing*, inspiring and humbling. It should drive us to be in worshipful awe of the most creative act there has ever been.

Father in Heaven, praise your name for deciding to create. Thank you for existence. Thank you for creating the universe. Thank you for creating me. Thank you for creating me with the ability reflect your creativity even in the smallest way. Lord, you did not have to create at all, but you decided to, and I thank you. Help me to see the beauty in creation even when I am wrestling with the meaning of life and existence itself. In the name of Jesus, Amen.

9

Without God Existence Could Not Exist

We have faith. So we understand that everything was made when God commanded it. That's why we believe that what we see was not made out of what could be seen. Abel had faith. So he brought to God a better offering than Cain did. Because of his faith Abel was praised as a godly man. God said good things about his offerings. Because of his faith Abel still speaks. He speaks even though he is dead. Enoch had faith. So he was taken from this life. He didn't die. "He couldn't be found, because God had taken him away." (Genesis 5:24) Before God took him, Enoch was praised as one who pleased God. Without faith it is impossible to please God. Those who come to God must believe that he exists. And they must believe that he rewards those who look to him.

~Hebrews 11:3–6 NIVR

"I believe in Christianity as I believe that the Sun has risen, not only because I see it but because by it, I see everything else."

~C.S. Lewis

"In God alone, essence (what He is) and existence (that he is) coincide."

~Avicenna

27

Everything observable in the universe is contingent. Nothing present at the big bang necessarily existed. Thus, time, matter, space, or energy did not have to exist. In fact, there is nothing necessary about the universe. The big bang, if assumed to be the singularity which birthed (time, space, matter, and energy) is contingent and not necessary, the singularity could not have created itself. Contingent things are never self-creating, self-sustaining, or self-sufficient. All contingent things have a cause. If the universe must have a cause because it is contingent, that cause must be God. Only God could be self-sufficient enough, powerful enough to create the universe. The universe must have been commanded to exist. God spoke (anthropomorphically analogously speaking), and existence began. Everything that is material and seen is contingent which gives evidence that it must have been created by one who is not seen. God commanded, and everything was made. Yes, this requires faith. We cannot prove God through our senses (through the objective world) as God is incorporeal (not material), but we can know God exists because existence itself exists. Light is incorporeal but we know light exists because we see everything by it. Creation itself (the material contingent universe) testifies to God's existence. Friends we can be confident that God exists because anything exists. Every sunrise is evidence for a loving creator. Just as by the light of the sun we see everything else, though we cannot see God may we see God's work in existence itself and allow it to testify and glorify God.

Father in Heaven you have made everything that is by your command. Without your creative will and power causing the universe there would be nothing at all. Existence itself is a mercy and act of love from you. Give me the faith to see you in your creation even though I cannot see you with my eyes. Give me the faith to bring the offering of my whole life and soul to your altar. Lord may my faith please you as Enoch's did. I know without faith I

cannot please you, so please give me the faith that does please you Lord. I believe you exist. Strengthen me by the evidence of your creation when I doubt your existence. Lord, I look to you for all hope. In Jesus name. Amen.

10

Left-Handed Lay Ups
and The Best of All Possible Worlds

"God saw everything he had made. And it was very good. There was evening, and there was morning. It was day six."
~Genesis 1:31 NIVR

"Now this supreme wisdom, united to a goodness that is no less infinite, cannot but have chosen the best. For as a lesser evil is a kind of good, even so, a lesser good is kind of evil if it stands in the way of a greater good; and there would be something to correct in the actions of God if it were possible to do better. As in mathematics, when there is no maximum nor minimum, in short nothing distinguished, everything is done equally, or when that is not possible nothing at all is done; so, it may be said likewise in respect to perfect wisdom, which is no less orderly than mathematics, that if there were not the best (optimum) among all possible worlds, God would not have produced any."
~Gottfried Wilhelm Leibniz

"This universe is simply a masterpiece of wisdom and order."
~ John Piper

That little adverb "very" puts emphasis on the fact that God didn't think the world was just good but *very* good. Philosopher and mathematician Gottfried Wilhelm Leibniz said this world (the one God chose to make) is the best of all possible worlds. God did not have to create at all. But if God is all-knowing, all-wise, and all-good he would not and could not create anything but the best version of existence possible. The issue is not one of limitations of power in and of itself but rather a limitation of power because of goodness. God could (and perhaps in terms of potentiality has in Leibniz description of possible worlds) create a less optimal cosmos, but because God is infinitely good, He would not.

Now this verse is of course before the fall of Adam and Eve and before sin entered the earth and humanity, but even before the fall the potentiality of the fall was there. Adam and Eve were given free will, and they could at any time choose to do what is not right and best. The best does not always mean perfect. To assume best and perfect are always the same is to make a mistake. This assumption calls into question either God's ability or judgment, but it does so based on the creation critiquing the creator. The reasons are good and perfect even if the situations are not, meaning they are from the most-wise choices. Sometimes the wisest thing I can do as a parent is to let my child work through an issue. My nine-year-old son loves two things; playing the drums and playing basketball. Drums comes easy for him, and he is quite gifted. He is a good little basketball player too, but it does not come easy for him. He has to work at it. He is a right-hand dominant player. He is not very good at left-handed lay ups, and it frustrates him to have to work on them. My son questions the wisdom of having to work on them. He does not always see the reason for it. He could just keep shooting with his right hand and shoot a much higher percentage. I could easily just tell him to not worry about it and to shoot all his layups with his right hand. That would in a way make my son's situation perfect, but it would not be the best. I know that as he grows, he will face players who will block his left-side layups if he doesn't learn to shoot them with his left hand. Plus, my son learns perseverance, work ethic, and even compassion for others by my allowing him to suffer through the learning process. I do not allow my son to be in what he would consider the perfect situation because in my wisdom I know it is not the best possible situation. Just like my son is learning to be the best basketball player he can be, we are all learning to be the people God intends for us to be. No the world is not perfect, but it is very good and perhaps very good is better than perfect.

Father in heaven, thank you for your wisdom. Thank you that I know when things are not perfected because there is an over-whelming amount of good to compare it to. Thank you for giving me so much good in my life that the imperfections of life stand out. Father help me to trust your wisdom. Thank you for caring about me enough to want me to develop into the person you intended me to be. In Jesus name. Amen.

11

The Reason and The Cause

The Lord wraps himself in light as if it were a robe. He spreads out the heavens like a tent.

~Psalm 104:2 NIVR

"Christians believe in the virgin birth of Jesus. Materialists believe in the virgin birth of the cosmos. Choose your miracle."

~Glen Scrivener

"Science proceeds by inference, rather than by the deduction of mathematical proof. A series of observations is accumulated, forcing the deeper question: What must be true if we are to explain what is observed? What "big picture" of reality offers the best fit to what is actually observed in our experience? American scientist and philosopher Charles S. Peirce used the term "abduction" to refer to the way in which scientists generate theories that might offer the best explanation of things. The method is now more often referred to as "inference to the best explanation." It is now widely agreed to be the philosophy of investigation of the world characteristic of the natural sciences."

~Alister E. McGrath

33

Which is the best explanation? Which requires more faith? That the materials that make up the universe (matter and energy) which are never self-creating did in fact at one point spring forth from pure potential only by chance and then form a universe that can sustain life all on its own, or perhaps that the big bang itself was directed by another. Was the cosmos a virgin birth so to speak, or was it the intentional act of a necessarily existing causal agent (i.e. God)? When I begin to doubt in the existence of God, I fall back on this—it seems to me a much smaller leap to believe the universe which appears to be directed in its birth and expansion and contains only that which does not have to exist was created by God (perhaps using the big bang as the way to create). This is a much smaller leap of faith than to believe the universe somehow created itself. Nothing present at the big bang necessarily existed. Thus, time, matter, space, or energy did not have to exist. In fact, there is nothing necessary about the universe. How can the universe itself have no cause when everything within the universe does have a cause?

Without a cause the origins of the universe are an infinite regress. This regression is analogous to a kid asking in infinitude, "But what was before that? What caused that?" Everything else in the universe has a cause, so why not the universe. If there is a cause then there must be a reason for that cause, if there is a reason for the universe to exist there is a reason for humans to exist. Since I know humans exist, it stands to reason humans exist to reflect the creator.

Psalm 104:2 says the Lord stretches out the heavens like a tent. This not only nods to the expansion of the universe (way before science discovered it… pretty cool that it did though), but also how the origins of the universe were an active creative endeavor of the will. The universe has a cause and a purpose. Therefore, each one of us humans have a first cause. Our parents are a secondary cause (we slip right back into the infinite regress going down the parent to grandparent to .... Adam and Eve). That first cause is God. You were intentionally made with a purpose. To believe that is to believe in something far more plausible than existence being happenstance and luck.

Father, you stretch out the heavens like a tent. You who made all that exists, you who made the universe seen and unseen, meet me in the dark when I begin to doubt you are there. Remind me that you are the best explanation for existence, and you are the only explanation that gives meaning to life. You give my life meaning. Praise your name that by you creating the universe, which is more vast than I can comprehend, gives my life intrinsic and unchanging meaning. In Jesus name. Amen

12

The Reason the Beginning Began

The Son is the exact likeness of God, who can't be seen. The Son is first, and he is over all creation. All things were created in him. He created everything in heaven and on earth. He created everything that can be seen and everything that can't be seen. He created kings, powers, rulers and authorities. All things have been created by him and for him. Before anything was created, he was already there. He holds everything together.
                                        ~Colossians 1: 15–17 NIVR

"It is certain, and obvious to the senses, that in the world some things are moved. But everything that is moved is moved by another."
    ~Thomas Aquinas (articulating Aristotelian thought)

"Therefore, since the ultimate ground must be in something which is of metaphysical necessity, and since the reason for an existing thing must come from something that actually exists, it follows that there must exist some one entity of metaphysical necessity, that is, there must be an entity whose essence is existence, and therefore something must exist which differs from the plurality of things,

which differs from the world, which we have granted and shown is not of metaphysical necessity."

~Gottfried Wilhelm Leibniz

For the natural to come to exist there must be something supernatural behind it causing that existence. A first cause. Leibniz determined this is a sufficient reason to assume that God exists. What Aristotle called a first mover and Aquinas called a first cause is needed before any secondary causes. Philosophically this all makes sense, but theologically what is a sufficient reason for God to have made the universe, humankind, you and me? Paul refers to God as the invisible God. This does not mean that the God of the Bible is a distant deist God, but it also doesn't mean that God can be anthropomorphically reduced to a giant wizard in the sky like in some Michelangelo painting either. What Paul means by God being invisible is that he is beyond nature. God is quite literally supernatural (beyond nature). So why then would a God who needed nothing create a natural universe (even the best and most wise universe)? Why does God, whose essence is existence itself, create by his own existence and then hold it together those is very own existence? The answer is, for himself. Now when we hear that it could seem quite selfish, but God whose essence is existence, before time began brought forth the universe into existence because it pleased him to create the universe, humankind… you and me.

In a very real sense, dare I say the most real, the beginning of existence began because it please God to make you so that he could love you and have relationship with you for all eternity. You were created for him. Yes, to serve him and please him, but even more to be loved by him.

Father in heaven, help me not to lose in my thoughts that before the universe and time began you already held me in your mind. Help me not to despair so much in my inability to fathom creation that I forget how my name was held in your love before you ever spoke, and matter burst forth. Help me to stay aware of how small and insignificant I am without you, but help me feel even in our most desperate and sinful days how infinitely and cosmically important I am because of you and your love for me. In the Holy name of Jesus, the only savior. Amen

13

Time Does Not Have God, God Has Time

"Jesus Christ is the same yesterday and today and forever."
~Hebrews 13:8 NIVR

"He is eternal, which means that He antedates time and is wholly independent of it. Time began in Him and will end in Him. To it He pays not tribute and from it He suffers no change."
~A.W. Tozer

"God exists outside of time, and since we are within time, there is no way we will ever totally grasp that concept."
~Francis Chan

Time does not have God, God has time (not only meaning that God has all the time he needs but that he possesses time itself). Time changes us. For those of us who are more well-seasoned than others, a quick glance at a mirror brings the harsh reality of the effects of time into focus (if our eyes can still focus). But God is not like us. God both precedes and proceeds time. What was there before the nothingness that was there before time began? What was before nothing, and what caused nothing to become something? One theory is that there once was nothing then Chuck Norris roundhouse kicked nothing and told it to get a job, and the universe sprang forth. Chuck Norris jokes aside, didn't something have to preexist what we describe as nothing for there to ever be something? The only answer possible is God.

This is such a comfort—if there is a God then he must both precede and proceed time and must therefore be unaffected by it. Love broke through the nothing, and we exist. The same Jesus who was there before time began is the same Jesus who took on flesh and humbled himself even to death on a cross. He is the same Jesus who now sits at the right hand of God the Father and with the Holy Spirit intercedes on our behalf. God (the Trinity) does not have to submit to time and remains the same yesterday, today, and forever. Friends, God's love and forgiveness for us is the same before the sins we committed yesterday, with us in the failures we may have today, and even in what may come tomorrow. We will fail, we will age, we will die, but Jesus will be there with us and for us through all of it just as he has always been.

Father God and Jesus, the son, you are eternal, unchanging, and free from time. You have loved me and planned for me before time began. Time cannot diminish your care and love for me. Time never speeds you up nor makes you too busy to hear my prayers and pleas. I praise your unchanging nature and your ever steady love. Even as I must submit to tomorrow, may I take refuge in the reality that tomorrow and every day after must submit to you. In the name of Jesus, Amen.

14

The Plan was Love

I now serve the good news because God gave me his grace. His power is at work in me. I am by far the least important of all the Lord's holy people. But he gave me the grace to preach to the Gentiles about the unlimited riches that Christ gives. God told me to make clear to everyone how the mystery came about. In times past it was kept hidden in the mind of God, who created all things. He wanted the rulers and authorities in the heavenly world to come to know his great wisdom. The church would make it known to them.

That was God's plan from the beginning. He has fulfilled his plan through Christ Jesus our Lord. Through him and through faith in him we can approach God. We can come to him freely. We can come without fear. So here is what I'm asking you to do. Don't lose hope because I am suffering for you. It will lead to the time when God will give you his glory.

~Ephesians 3:7–13 NIVR

"Creation discloses a power that baffles our minds and beggars our speech. We are enamored and enchanted by God's power. We stutter and stammer about God's holiness. We tremble before God's majesty...and yet, we grow squeamish and skittish before God's love."

~Brennan Manning

"How could anything rightly be said about love if you were forgotten. God of love, from whom all love comes in heaven and on earth; You who held nothing back but did give everything in love; You who are love, so the lover is only what he is through being in you."

~Soren Kierkegaard

If we trust our senses at all, we know that existence does in fact exist. Even though we are all limited in that we are each one person with one perspective, we have a shared world we live in. That there is existence does not tend to bother us, but why existence exists tends to be a different story. What does it all mean is a question humans have asked since we could ask questions? Why did God create at all? For what purpose?

Paul tells us in Ephesians the reasons God chose to create. First God chose to create so his great wisdom would be known not just by humans but all creation (v.9–10). God created to demonstrate his wisdom. Now to clarify, God did not *need* to be known. God has no need, but he *wanted* to be known. Second, God wanted not only to create humans but made a way to draw us close. This could only be done through Jesus and his death and resurrection (v.11). God chose to create free beings with free will which always leaves the potential for sin. Jesus was the way to reconcile God's great gift of free will to humans with his desire for us to be close to him. God created to be known. Finally, God created to be glorified and for those who give their lives to him to be glorified in him (v. 13). God created to be glorified and to glorify through the reconciling grace of the good news (v.7).

God created for the purpose of demonstrating his wisdom, to be known, and to be glorified by reconciling us to him. All these purposes funnel into this; God created because he is love and he loves us so much. For God loved the world in this way, that he gave his only son (John 3:16). Existence exists so that God can love us and have relationship with us. This is possible through the unlimited riches of the good news.

Father in heaven, thank you for your love. Help me to become so boldly comfortable in knowing you created with the purpose of loving me that it is absolute synonymous with my identity. I am the beloved. Lord, may knowing that I am the beloved make me ever more bold and comfortable making your name known in the world around me. Father, thank you for the grace and gift of my free will even when I freely choose my will over yours. Help me recognize the choice as a gift of your grace. Jesus thank you for your obedience to the Father in coming to earth to reconcile me a sinner to you. Jesus thank you for the unlimited riches you give to me. Holy Spirit strengthen me and guide me to choose holiness and righteousness when exercising my free choices. Father, may I seek to see your wisdom in all creation, in existence itself and through your holy word. Help me to know you and to be known by you. May my life bring you glory, and may I glory in you in every circumstance. In Jesus name. Amen.

Part 2

15

Peter's Worldview: Deconstruction And Reconstruction

Jesus went to the area of Caesarea Philippi. There he asked his disciples, "Who do people say the Son of Man is?"

They replied, "Some say John the Baptist. Others say Elijah. Still others say Jeremiah, or one of the prophets."

"But what about you?" he asked. "Who do you say I am?"

Simon Peter answered, "You are the Messiah. You are the Son of the living God."

Jesus replied, "Blessed are you, Simon, son of Jonah! No mere human showed this to you. My Father in heaven showed it to you. Here is what I tell you. You are Peter. On this rock I will build my church. The gates of hell will not be strong enough to destroy it.

~Matthew 16:13–18 NIVR

Jesus then began to teach his disciples. He taught them that the Son of Man must suffer many things. He taught them that the elders would not accept him. The chief priests and the teachers of the law would not accept him either. He must be killed and after three days rise again. He spoke clearly about this. Peter took Jesus to one side and began to scold him.

46

Jesus turned and looked at his disciples. He scolded Peter. "Get behind me, Satan!" he said. "You are not thinking about the things God cares about. Instead, you are thinking only about the things humans care about."

~Mark 8:31–33 NIVR

Simon Peter had a sword and pulled it out. He struck the high priest's slave and cut off his right ear. The slave's name was Malchus.

~John 18:10 NIVR

Peter said, "Brothers and sisters, a long time ago the Holy Spirit spoke through David. He spoke about Judas Iscariot. What the Scripture said would happen had to come true. Judas was the guide for the men who arrested Jesus.

~Acts 1:16 NIVR

"My fellow Israelites, I know you didn't realize what you were doing. Neither did your leaders. But God had given a promise through all the prophets. And this is how he has made his promise come true. He said that his Messiah would suffer. So, turn away from your sins. Turn to God. Then your sins will be wiped away.

The time will come when the Lord will make everything new. He will send the Messiah. Jesus has been appointed as the Messiah for you. Heaven must receive him until the time when God makes everything new. He promised this long ago through his holy prophets.

Moses said, 'The Lord your God will raise up for you a prophet like me. He will be one of your own people. You must listen to everything he tells you. Anyone who does not listen to him will be completely cut off from their people.' (Deuteronomy 18:15,18,19)

~Acts 3:17–23 NIVR

"We know not through our intellect but through our experience."

~Maurice Merleau-Ponty

Used to be I'd only get born again about every year—once a year. That was when I was going to camp… those of you that are young enough to go to camp and re-dedicate your life every year, you keep doing it, 'cause about the time you get to college you're gonna learn that you have to re-dedicate your life about every six months. And then you'll graduate from college, and it will become a quarterly thing. By the time you're in your forties and fifties you'll do it four times a day."

~Rich Mullins

When I was in high school if someone would have approached me and offered me a meal of glutinous grass seed, ocean algae, and uncooked aquatic meat, I would have not only politely declined the offer but most likely would have vomited in my mouth a little as I declined. But now sushi is by far my favorite meal. I would eat sushi for every meal if I could afford it (and if that whole mercury poisoning thing weren't a thing). I have deconstructed from what I assumed sushi would taste like to what I know now is the most delicious food there is. What I expected did not match reality. The only way for me to discover this was to encounter the dialectic move of encountering information that rubbed against my limited worldview.

In college a friend of mine whom I knew wasn't weird or crazy told me sushi was delicious. This information was the antithesis to my thesis of the world at the time. I decided to give it a try and reached a new synthesis. I expanded my pallet and in turn my worldview. If I did not deconstruct from my worldview of assuming sushi would be nasty and try it, I would have never reached a higher synthesis. If I never tried sushi, I would have missed out on my favorite food. My worldview would not include one of my favorite things.

According to the *Cambridge Encyclopedia of Philosophy* deconstruction is, "a demonstration of the incompleteness or incoherence of a philosophical position using concepts and principles of argument whose meaning and use is legitimated only by that philosophical position." Philosophically the term deconstruction gained prominence in the work of postmodern French philosopher Jacques Derrida. Derrida's basic premise is that meaning cannot be fully shared because meaning is not repeatable and further language is inadequate to fully comprehend and communicate meanings (in this regard his thoughts align with Thomas Aquinas). Philosophically deconstruction is about ridding oneself of presuppositions. In plain language deconstruction is putting an assumed belief back on the table for reexamination. Deconstruction for the purpose of gaining a better understanding of true orthodoxy of our belief system is a good thing. We all deconstruct all the time. If you are married and have found yourself converting on a particular brand of mustard or ketchup you have deconstructed. If your spouse has shown which way the toothpaste tube should be rolled, you have deconstructed. You have then reconstructed into a new higher synthesized worldview when it comes to toothpaste.

In the case of Peter (and Jews as a nation), he had a worldview in which the expectation was that the Messiah would be a military and political savior. The Jews blended nationalism with their faith (sound familiar America?) and this diluted, confused, and jumbled God's promise of a Messiah. Peter expected a Maccabean Messiah like Judah the Hammer who would incite a military uprising to fight oppressive political policies against the Jews by an occupying nation. Jesus was nothing like Judah Maccabees. Jesus never intended any sort of military or political revolt but rather a heart and soul revolution. Peter's worldview was too small. Peter needed to reach a new and higher synthesis.

Friends we can see in the passages outlined above that early on Peter (Simon) recognized Jesus as Messiah. It was this recognition that prompted Jesus to changed Simon's name to Peter. Now whether the "Rock" was the person of Simon or simply the truth of the declaration that Jesus was the Messiah who knows, but even though Peter knew Jesus was the Messiah his understanding of what the Messiah was to be needed deconstruction and reconstruction.

Peter rebuked Jesus for saying that he must suffer. Peter was still expecting Jesus to eventually kick butt and take names so to speak. Jesus in turn tells Peter his worldview is too small and only concerned with human issues (and particularly Jewish national concerns). But we see in Acts after Jesus' death and resurrection Peter's worldview of what the Messiah would be has been expanded and reconstructed. Peter says Jesus' betrayal by Judas and death had to happen. Peter realized the Messiah had to die, there would be no military revolt, and that was never God's plan. In fact, this was how God "fulfilled what he had foretold" saying that the "Messiah would suffer." Peter who rebuked Jesus for saying he had to suffer was now telling others the Messiah had to suffer. This is a complete deconstruction and reconstruction into a higher synthesis of Peter's belief system. Peter now has expanded his worldview and synthesized that the Messiah coming was bigger than a revolt against an occupying nation. It was the revolution of restoration for all of creation and for salvation to come not just to the Jews but to all who would call upon the name of Jesus.

Friends we all deconstruct our beliefs all the time. We are on a journey. If you see yourself in Peter, take heart. Jesus will cause us to deconstruct our often too small worldviews and expand them into his reality. God's plan isn't limited to our worldview or our understanding, but he is faithful to walk with us and shape our worldviews to come closer and closer to his if we just continue to follow him.

Father God thank you for showing me Peter's failures and frailty, his limited understanding, and his rash proclamations because I see so much of myself in him. But even more Lord thank you for how you transformed Peter into the leader he became. Thank you for breaking apart his wrong assumptions and expanding his worldview. Let me be encouraged and humbly submit to the Holy Spirit doing the same deconstruction in my lives when what I assume does not match your truth, Lord. Change me in all the ways I differ from you. I long to be like you, Lord. Thank you for being faithful to shape me into your image. Thank you that you love me too much to leave me as I am. In Jesus name. Amen.

16

Paul Reasoned with the Athenians

While Paul was waiting for them in Athens, he was greatly distressed to see that the city was full of idols. So he reasoned in the synagogue with both Jews and God-fearing Greeks, as well as in the marketplace day by day with those who happened to be there.

A group of Epicurean and Stoic philosophers began to debate with him. Some of them asked, "What is this babbler trying to say?" Others remarked, "He seems to be advocating foreign gods." They said this because Paul was preaching the good news about Jesus and the resurrection. Then they took him and brought him to a meeting of the Areopagus, where they said to him, "May we know what this new teaching is that you are presenting? You are bringing some strange ideas to our ears, and we would like to know what they mean." (All the Athenians and the foreigners who lived there spent their time doing nothing but talking about and listening to the latest ideas.)

Paul then stood up in the meeting of the Areopagus and said: "People of Athens! I see that in every way you are very religious. For as I walked around and looked carefully at your objects of worship, I even found an altar with this inscription: TO AN UNKNOWN GOD. So, you are ignorant of the very thing you worship—and this is what I am going to proclaim to you.

"The God who made the world and everything in it is the Lord of heaven and earth and does not live in temples built by human hands. And he is not served by human hands, as if he needed anything. Rather, he himself gives everyone life and breath and everything else. From one man he made all the nations, that they should inhabit the whole earth; and he marked out their appointed times in history and the boundaries of their lands.

"God did this so that they would seek him and perhaps reach out for him and find him, though he is not far from any one of us. 'For in him we live and move and have our being.' As some of your own poets have said, 'We are his offspring.'

"Therefore, since we are God's offspring, we should not think that the divine being is like gold or silver or stone—an image made by human design and skill. In the past God overlooked such ignorance, but now he commands all people everywhere to repent. For he has set a day when he will judge the world with justice by the man he has appointed. He has given proof of this to everyone by raising him from the dead."

When they heard about the resurrection of the dead, some of them sneered, but others said, "We want to hear you again on this subject." At that, Paul left the Council. Some of the people became followers of Paul and believed. Among them was Dionysius, a member of the Areopagus, also a woman named Damaris, and a number of others.

~Acts 17:16–34 NIV

"To scorn the dictate of reason is to scorn the commandment of God."

~Thomas Aquinas

"Reason is our starting point. There can be no question either of attacking or defending it."

~C.S. Lewis

Friends in this fascinating passage we see Paul in the most important city in ancient Greece. Paul studies and engages the culture. Before Paul could challenge their worldview, he had to understand their worldview. Paul then uses reason in the context of Athenian culture to contend for the gospel. Paul does not tell Jews or Greeks in the broader culture just to believe but rather uses his intellect and logic as a tool for the gospel. In Christianity we are not asked to check our brains at the door but rather to engage our intellect and hearing from the Holy Spirit with the cultural philosophies and worldviews we find ourselves encountering. Paul was not ignorant of the predominant worldview of the Athenian culture of the day. He learned the cultural zeitgeists of the people; how they thought. He was a student of the culture and the worldviews birthed from that culture.

Paul translated the gospel so it could be heard, understood, and appropriated to their culture, in the way they think. Yet he did not water-down or shy away from the gospel. He translated to their culture *but he did not change the gospel.* He did not progressive-ize the gospel. Here is some ways Paul engaged with the Areopagite (a council of advisors).

1. He complimented their faithfulness to their religion
2. He let them know he had studied their culture
3. He told them the God they admit they did not know could be known. He was using their beliefs as an entrance for the gospel
4. He proclaimed the one true God.
5. He quoted one of their poets. He again used their cultural references to present the gospel.
6. He called for repentance in light of God's justice.
7. He gave evidence by pointing to the physical death and resurrection of Jesus.
8. Then he left.

The text says two people converted to Christianity that day.

Friends, in this example Paul gives us, we can see that we can use reason as a tool to contend for Jesus. We should not scorn the dictate of reason but rather see it as another gift of God. We cannot be afraid to study those who are not believers and to use our intellect to interpret (with the Holy Spirit) the cultural context into a gospel message.

Father God, thank you for the gift of reason. Thank you that your transcendent truth can be seen and used at all times, in all cultures and every worldview for your glory. May I become an expert at understanding the philosophies and worldviews of my culture so that I know how to best engage those around me with the one true gospel—that of the death, resurrection, and sacrificial atonement of your only son Jesus Christ for the forgiveness of sins for all that will believe. Lord help me see how to use the culture as a tool and to not be afraid to speak boldly when I do see. Forgive me for the times I have been ignorant or fearful and remained silent when I should have spoken. Forgive me for the times I may have spoken when I should have stayed silent. Give me your wisdom in all circumstances. Your gospel won't be stopped. Thank you for letting me play a small role in spreading it. In Jesus name. Amen

17

What is Truth?

Pilate then went back inside the palace, summoned Jesus and asked him, "Are you the king of the Jews?"

"Is that your own idea," Jesus asked, "or did others talk to you about me?"

"Am I a Jew?" Pilate replied. "Your own people and chief priests handed you over to me. What is it you have done?"

Jesus said, "My kingdom is not of this world. If it were, my servants would fight to prevent my arrest by the Jewish leaders. But now my kingdom is from another place."

"You are a king, then!" said Pilate.

Jesus answered, "You say that I am a king. In fact, the reason I was born and came into the world is to testify to the truth. Everyone on the side of truth listens to me."

"What is truth?" retorted Pilate. With this he went out again to the Jews gathered there and said, "I find no basis for a charge against him. But it is your custom for me to release to you one prisoner at the time of the Passover. Do you want me to release 'the king of the Jews'?"

~John 18: 33–39 NIV

"Jesus answered, "I am the way and the truth and the life. No

56

one comes to the Father except through me."

~John 14:6 NIV

"People love truth when it shines warmly on them and hate it when it rebukes them."

~Augustine

"I will never know how you see red and you will never know how I see it. But this separation of consciousness is recognized only after a failure of communication, and our first movement is to believe in an undivided being between us."

~Maurice Merleau-Ponty

Your worldview and sense of self provide much of the instruction manual for how you see truth. Someone who holds a material naturalist view of the world will see truth much more from an objective standpoint. Truth to the naturalist is that which is observable and can be measured. While someone with a relativist worldview will obviously view truth as relative. Someone with a postmodern or existentialist worldview will be far more likely to view truth from a subjective standpoint. Someone with a religious worldview is far more likely to see truth as transcendent or divinely revealed.

All worldviews give priority and are biased to a certain view of truth. In this passage Pilate is revealing how he viewed truth. He simultaneously reveals that he believed truth cannot be known and it wouldn't matter if it could be known. In other words, Pilate places little value on truth.

The philosophies of modernity (17th through early 20th centuries) reduced truth to only that which can be seen, observed, and measured. Post-modernity (second half of the 20th century) seeing the flaws in modernity reduced truth as purely subjective and only relative to the experience of the individual. In the postmodern reduction of truth, it always shined warmly on the individual because it was only subject to the individual. Both modernity and post-modernity over-emphasized one kind of truth and dismissed all others. Neither of these are a Christian view of truth. The truth is complex and robust. We do interact with an objective world, and we communicate about it analogously with each other in our intersubjectivity but never in a completely univocal way for two primary reasons:

1. The world/universe in inexhaustible. We will never fully understand nor be able to communicate the universe to one another. This does not mean there is no knowledge or that knowledge cannot be communicated at all.

2. We are contained by the nature of being a subjective self. Our experience of truth will never fully coincide with another subjective self's interaction with it. This does not mean there is not truth, only that we each interact with truth as ourselves and thus we can never communicate it wholly to one another.

We all see in part and know in part... all of us encounter objective truth but never objectively. We are trapped in our experience of objective reality. Christianity does not reduce truth to a singular kind of truth (relative or objective) but rather includes both, and it demands a response from humans to the whole truth. The whole truth rebukes us and reminds us of our limited knowledge and ability to truly understand truth. Yet there it is roaring at us, demanding we deal with and prioritize it. Truth is objective and subjective and intersubjective and relative and transcendent. So, what is truth? How can it be known? By the only one who can know objective reality and each individual's truth and each individual's interactions with each other and the transcendent supernatural truth. In other words, God is truth. Friends, the whole truth unreduced can only be found in Jesus Christ. When Pilate asked "what is truth" he was asking the question to truth itself. He was asking the question to the great "I am."

Father God, ultimate reality, the whole truth is only contained and can only be known by you. You are truth itself and its source. Help me to seek truth in you and you alone. Holy Spirit guide me in increasingly understanding truth and protect me from outright falsities. Protect me even from slight drifts from truth, from you. Keep me in a spirit of humility in knowing I am one person experiencing the world and you Lord only from my perspective when dealing with my brothers and sisters. Help me to learn from them so that I may know you better. Jesus you are my example, my savior, and my king. May I never take my eyes off you... the truth. In Jesus' name. Amen

18

A Hip with a Limp:
Wrestling with your Worldview

That night Jacob got up and took his two wives, his two female servants, and his eleven sons and crossed the ford of the Jabbok. After he had sent them across the stream, he sent over all his possessions.

So, Jacob was left alone, and a man wrestled with him till daybreak. When the man saw that he could not overpower him, he touched the socket of Jacob's hip so that his hip was wrenched as he wrestled with the man.

Then the man said, "Let me go, for it is daybreak."

But Jacob replied, "I will not let you go unless you bless me."

The man asked him, "What is your name?"

"Jacob," he answered.

Then the man said, "Your name will no longer be Jacob, but Israel, because you have struggled with God and with humans and have overcome."

Jacob said, "Please tell me your name."

But he replied, "Why do you ask my name?" Then he blessed him there.

So Jacob called the place Peniel, saying, "It is because I saw God face to face, and yet my life was spared."

The sun rose above him as he passed Peniel and he was limp-ing because of his hip.

~Genesis 32:22–31 NIV

"In Love's service, only wounded soldiers can serve."

~Brennan Manning

"Rather than unfairly asking only religious people to prove their views, we need to compare and contrast religious beliefs and their evidences with secular beliefs and theirs. We can and should argue about which beliefs account for what we see and experience in the world. We can and should debate the inner logical consistency of belief systems, asking whether they support or contradict one another. We can and should consult our deepest intuitions."

~Tim Keller

I used to play basketball four or five days a week and then would go on long distance runs on the days I did not play basket-ball. About five years ago while training for a marathon, I began to experience abdomen pain. I first thought it was a pulled muscle, then after it persisted, I thought maybe it was an appendix issue. I took a few weeks off to see if that would help. It did not. I decided I just needed to man up through it while it healed and continue in my exercise routine. I was the guy who played an entire basketball season on a broken ankle. I have always had crazy pain tolerance and honestly took pride in it (my dad was a rugby player after all… no wimps in this family) so I thought this would be no different—just keep going and it will eventually heal. Three years later and it just kept getting worse. I had to stop running, stop playing basketball, and finally go see a doctor. I ended up finding out I had a 90% torn labrum and severe cartilage damage that required major surgery.

61

I had the surgery, and while I was under the knife the surgeon discovered I was in even worse condition than he originally thought. He had to repair the labrum, clean out bone fragments and torn cartilage, and he had to shave the bones of my hip socket and femur. What originally was projected to be a three-month recovery turned into a year. My pride in my ability to ignore pain turned into embarrassment of my stubbornness.

Post-surgery I needed help with daily tasks like taking a shower, getting into a car, etc. It was humbling. While I no longer walk with a limp, and I am back playing basketball a couple of days a week. I had to give distance running up. I must be careful and stretch. I still feel it even now. That hip is weaker… and always will be.

I learned I needed to lean on my wife and kids to help take care of me after my surgery. If I am honest, I hated it. I was wounded physically, but the real surgery was the Lord removing the tumor of my pride. I was angry at times with God about this, but I also knew I had to lean into it and onto him in much the same way I had to lean onto my wife to get in and out of a car.

Jacob early in life had his own issues with pride. His worldview was very self-centered. This is not Jacob's first encounter with a blessing. The first time Jacob stole his father's blessing from his twin brother and then suffered the humiliation of having to run for his life from that brother. Jacob deceived his father to get that blessing and then was deceived by his wives' father who tricked Jacob into marrying the sister he was not pursuing. Jacob had been humbled.

This time Jacob knew he had to hang in there and fight for his blessing, and he was not going to let go until he received it from the Lord the right way. The younger prideful Jacob would have tried to find a short cut, but now an older humbled Jacob knew there were no short cuts. There was no ignoring the pain.

Friends, like Jacob I have learned from my own humiliation and having a hip with a limp that our wounds keep our pride in check and our hearts tender for the suffering of others. But mostly our limps remind us of our dependence on God. Not only for physical health but spiritual as well.

Father in heaven thank you for my wounds and weaknesses. For it is those very things that keep me from thinking I have it all together. Scars remind me that I need you. A limp removes any deception that I am anything but utterly dependent upon the grace and mercy of Jesus Christ. Lord use my weakness and failings to draw my heart's attention to you and also my fellow human travelers. Help my limp help to spur me to see the wounds of others as an opportunity to be a soldier in love's service. In the name of Jesus Christ. Amen.

19

The Self

"*Therefore, we do not lose heart. Though outwardly we are wasting away, yet inwardly we are being renewed day by day.*"

~2 Corinthians 4:16 NIV

"*A human being is spirit. But what is spirit? Spirit is the self. But what is the self? The self is a relation that relates itself to itself or is the relation's relating itself to itself in the relation; the self is not the relation but is the relation's relating itself to itself. A human being is a synthesis of the infinite and the finite, of the temporal and the eternal, of freedom and necessity, in short, a synthesis.*"

~Soren Kierkegaard

"Humans are amphibians...half spirit and half animal... as spirits they belong to the eternal world, but as animals they inhabit time. This means that while their spirit can be directed to an eternal object, their bodies, passions, and imaginations are in continual change, for to be in time, means to change."

~C.S. Lewis

Who am I? That is question humans have asked since we began to ask questions. There is a question behind that question of "who am I?" The more foundational question is what it means to be an "I." What does it mean to be a self?

If he soul is a farce, then so is the self. How can that mammal reasonably use first-person pronouns? Scientifically and philosophically, there is no "I" or "me," the individual is not real. Only the physical matter of "I" that is leading "me" to believe there is "I" (a "me" the material naturalist denies is real); "I" does not exist. "My" brain is lying to "me." "I" has no mind. In other words, material naturalism eliminates the idea of the self by which all humans daily operate. The naturalist believes the soul is merely a construct of the brain. Without the metaphysical, there is no self…there is no person.

My self is either a metaphysical, supernatural reality or it does not exist at all. The self, the "I" either exists outside the confines of the body, the brain, and even consciousness or it does not exist at all. If the self can be reduced to consciousness, then every time I go to sleep or have anesthesia, I am not a self. Or more gravely, babies and invalids are not "selves."

Christianity teaches that the self is transcendent and made in the image of God. Even though we are beyond the physical, we experience ourselves as an embodied soul. The entire human experience is as an embodied soul. That body is all we know of existing. We have always been an embodied soul, and that body is wasting away. But humans can never be reduced to that which is wasting away.

Friends, our essence is spirit, supernatural, and made in the image of God, but an essence that is eternally intended and operates optimally as embodied. For those who trust in Jesus for salvation, our "selves" will live in eternity united to him. That is good news.

Father God, thank you for making me, me. Thank you that I

am more than this body which will decay and die. Lord what a gift it is to have a body and that I am to steward it well, but you have made me more than a body. Thank you for making me in your image in this way. In this union of the finite and infinite help me to use the time wisely but for it to be ever present that I am made for eternity with you. In Jesus name. Amen.

20

Finding your Self by Denying Yourself

Then Jesus said to his disciples, "Whoever wants to be my disciple must deny themselves and take up their cross and follow me. For whoever wants to save their life will lose it, but whoever loses their life for me will find it. What good will it be for someone to gain the whole world, yet forfeit their soul? Or what can anyone give in exchange for their soul? For the Son of Man is going to come in his Father's glory with his angels, and then he will reward each person according to what they have done. "Truly I tell you, some who are standing here will not taste death before they see the Son of Man coming in his kingdom."
~Matthew 16:24–28 NIV

"There is within the human heart a tough fibrous root of fallen life whose nature is to possess, always to possess. It covets "things" with a deep and fierce passion. The pronouns 'my' and 'mine' look innocent enough in print, but their constant and universal use is significant.… They are verbal symptoms of our deep disease."

~A.W. Tozer

"You have made us for yourself, O Lord, and our heart

is restless until it rests in you."

~Augustine

The concept and essence of the self as a metaphysical, supernatural reality means that self is intrinsically immutably necessarily found in God and God alone. Therefore, to truly understand ourselves, to find our true selves, our identity, we must deny our own concepts of ourselves. To become understood by others and to understand ourselves we must reject the world and others' ideas of who we are. By losing and giving up our self-conception of who we are and replacing that with God's definition of who we are, we end up finding our true selves because God made us for himself and to be found, understood in Him. To become who we are meant to be, we are meant to strive to replace our concepts of who we are with who God says we are. God is the giver of self and created humans in his image, so he is the prototype for us. Friends, the one who made us is the only one who can define us. He defines us as truly, deeply, completely loved and valued by him.

This takes all the pressure off us to carve out an identity. We can simply accept how loved and accepted we are by the one who made us a "self" in the first place. This is good news.

Friends the greatest gift God gives is salvation through the death and resurrection of his son Jesus for the forgiveness of sins. The second greatest gift after salvation that God ever gives somebody is getting over themselves. Now we must be a self to get over ourselves, but an immensely vital part of Christianity is getting over yourself.

Father God, help me to find myself in you alone. Lord, I deny myself today. Holy Spirit help me to deny myself today and take up my cross. Help me to choose to deny myself every day. I repent for the times I fail and let my own flawed concept of myself supersede who you say I am. Forgive me for when, like a child, I replace you Jesus for "my" and "mine." Lord, I reject the lie of who I tell

myself I am, and I reject even more the lie of who the world tells me I am. Most of all I reject the lies of who the enemy tells me I am. Lord, you tell me I am one who is infinitely loved, honored, and accepted by you even when I choose myself and fail you. Lord keep me from sin, but when I do sin help me not to believe that defines who I am. Make me holy in my behavior, Lord, but even more in my heart by accepting my true self as only being found in you and your salvation. In Jesus name. Amen.

21

How Will the World Know we Follow Him?

"A new command I give you: Love one another. As I have loved you, so you must love one another. By this everyone will know that you are my disciples, if you love one another.
~John 13:34–35 NIV

Jesus replied: "Love the Lord your God with all your heart and with all your soul and with all your mind.' This is the first and greatest commandment. And the second is like it: 'Love your neighbor as yourself.' All the Law and the Prophets hang on these two commandments."
~Matthew 22:37–40 NIV

This is how we know what love is: Jesus Christ laid down his life for us. And we ought to lay down our lives for our brothers and sisters.
~1 John 3:16 NIV

Love is patient, love is kind. It does not envy, it does not boast, it is not proud. It does not dishonor others, it is not self-seeking, it is not easily angered, it keeps no record of wrongs. Love does not delight in evil but rejoices with the truth. It always protects,

always trusts, always hopes, always perseveres.
~1 Corinthians 13:4–7 NIV

"A people is an assemblage of reasonable beings bound together by common agreement as to the objects of their love, then, in order to discover the character of any people, we have only to observe what they love."
~Saint Augustine

"To love another in spite of his weaknesses and errors and imperfections is not perfect love. No, to love is to find him lovable in spite of and together with his weakness and errors and imperfections."
~Soren Kierkegaard

If the creator created out of love, then perhaps the chief end of humanity is to love. Human awareness of that mission and the ability to choose to live it out is what makes humans particular. Deep-down humans long for meaning and purpose. Humans desire to know why we exist. Humans have the will, volition, and opportunity to choose to love or to choose not to love. Jesus says meaning is found in love. First that we love God with everything we have in us. Friends that means that we are to love God above ourselves, our spouse, our children, our parents—everyone. But then we are to love each other just as we do ourselves. In fact, Jesus says the greatest evangelical tool Christians have is not sound doctrine, not great worship music, not clever sermons, not feeding the hungry, not miracles and healing, not charity, not even loving our enemies. All of these are good and righteous, but none of them is the Christian's greatest attractional tool. What will let the world know we have something they want (and what we have is the gospel of Jesus Christ) is our love for each other.

Friends, Augustine says to know a people you only have to look

71

at what they love. We should be loving God first. It seems to me a lot of Christians get this right. But then we are to love one another. How well does the Church (not your church or my church but THE church) do in loving one another? We should follow the example of Jesus and the apostles in loving one another. Not that there won't be disagreement, there will be. I mean Paul and Barnabas got into a bit of a brouhaha, and Peter and Paul got into a disagreement as well in Acts, but they were committed to working it out and loving one another. We should follow their example. Love is more than utility. Love is more than kindness; love is more than a feeling (and more than an old classic rock song by Boston). Love is the ultimate ethic. The world (both next door and across the globe) will be softened to the gospel when they see Christians (within each church and between churches) who are patient and kind to one another, who are humble with one another, who forgive one another 70x7 time and then again, who value truth over their own agenda or opinion, and who don't give up on one another no matter how bad it gets. Friends, the better we get at loving one another, the more the world will realize that we have the truth of the gospel and will want Jesus in their lives.

Father, help us believers to love one another truly and deeply. Help me to love the person in the seat next to me in church and the church down the street. Help me to stand for the truth of the gospel never compromising it, but to let all else that divides me from other Christians go. Help me to let go of biases, preferences, and prejudices that have nothing to do with the gospel. Bring a deep conviction to my heart to commit to living out 1 Corinthians 13 in my interactions with other believers from my own church but also from other denominations, traditions, and cultures. Help me to see the catholic (small c) church as one body and bride. Lord no loving husband adores his wife's eyes but hates her fingers. Just as you love all of your bride, help me to love all of your bride as well so that the world may know I follow no one but you Jesus. In your holy name. Amen.

Part 3

22

Natural Evil and Human Understanding

"Where were you when I laid the earth's foundation? Tell me, if you understand. Who marked off its dimensions? Surely you know! Who stretched a measuring line across it? On what were its footings set, or who laid its cornerstone—while the morning stars sang together and all the angels[a] shouted for joy?"
~Job 38:4–7 NIV

"The sea is not less beautiful in our eyes because we know that ships are sometimes wrecked by it. If it altered the movement of its waves to spare a ship it would be a creature gifted with discernment and choice, and not this fluid perfectly obedient to every external power. It is this obedience which makes the sea's beauty."
~Simone Weil

"An artist produces two paintings, one of which is large in order to serve as a model for a tapestry, while the other is only a miniature. Let us take the miniature one and say that there are two things to consider in it; firstly, its positive and real aspect, which consists of the board, the background, the colors, and the brushstrokes; and secondly, its privative

74

aspect, which is the disproportion to the large painting, or its smallness. Therefore, it would be absurd to say that the artist is the author of all that is real in the two paintings, without also being the author of the privative, or of the disproportion between the large one and the small one. For by the same reason, or rather by a stronger reason, one could say that an artist can be the author of a copy or of a portrait, i.e. without being the author of this flaw. For, in fact, the privative is nothing other than a simple result or infallible consequence of the positive and does not require a separate author."

~Gottfried Wilhelm Leibniz

Friends, imagine we have all walked into a music venue and heard someone scream "Free Bird" or "Wagon Wheel" at the poor musician trying to play us their newest original song. Eventually when the musician is either enticed by a hefty tip or bullied by the incessant moronic demands of those calling for "Freebird" and acquiesces, we don't get confused on who the author of the song is. We know the musician playing "Free Bird," "Wagon Wheel," or "Tennessee Whiskey" is not the songwriter. We all know this is a cover song. No matter what changes to the arrangement or missed chords, no matter how fast or slow the song is played, we all know the copyright of the song does not change hands.

There are two types of evil in the world that bring about suffering; natural evil and moral evil. Moral evil is the result of human actions. Either our own free will or the free will of others. Natural evil is evil that cannot be attributed to human action. Natural evil (such as hurricanes, earthquakes, even non-human caused death itself) can only be attributed to nature itself or the action of divine beings. Analytic philosopher Alvin Plantinga asserts that it is possible that there are divine beings (angels, demons, Satan) that have free will as well, and it is possible natural evil can be attributed to them. Others simply define natural evil as evil that is void or independent of human intervention.

A little over a year ago our family dog of twelve years had to be put down as cancer had overtaken her body. Our wolf hybrid (Tundra—75% German Shepherd and 25% Timberwolf) was the most amazing, loyal, and loving pet I have ever owned. It was devastating to our family. Her death was a natural part of life, but both her suffering and ours didn't make sense. On some level suffering never makes sense. Suffering always stings of something being off. Is that sting evidence that God is guilty of or complicit in suffering, or is it a sign to humanity that existence itself is not as it was intended to be?

Friends, humans don't have the epistemic access to know why suffering happens—particularly suffering from natural evil. What did my dog directly do to deserve cancer? Her cancer was not due to any direct moral failing. It and her death were a result of natural evil. The best biblical example of this is Job. Job was a righteous man by all accounts. Now we know he was a sinner because all humans are sinners, but the loss Job suffered was not because of his actions nor the actions of other humans. Job's suffering was due to a conversation between Satan and God. Job's suffering was supernaturally permitted but naturally executed. Job lost his wealth, his health, his children, his wife, and his friends. Job asks God, as we often do, why he had to suffer like he did. Job didn't understand, and he wanted an explanation. God responded with *where were you when I created creation?* In other words, *who are you to ask me to explain myself?* This may seem harsh, but perhaps it would not relieve Job's suffering even if God would have explained. Job (and we) may not be able to understand why even if the reasons why were given.

There is always something off about suffering. The world was created to be perfect, but perhaps perfect is not what was best.

God made creation perfect, but he also made beings with free will. When sin entered creation (whether you think that is when Satan and the angels chose sin or when Adam and Eve chose sin)

76

all of creation fell. This means we live in a natural world that is a cover of the original. We live in a creation that has beauty, but the cover is never as good as the original. That guy in the bar playing "Free Bird" never plays it quite as good as Lynyrd Skynyrd, yet that does not mean it can't be enjoyed, just that there is always something off about it. Just as we don't blame Lynyrd Skynyrd for the flaws in the cover, we should not blame God for the natural evil that is the result of sin.

Father in heaven, help me to trust you amid suffering. Help me not to blame you for the natural evils in the world but to turn to you for my comfort and my sustenance. Lord help me to trust you in the darkness as I do in the light. Help me to have joy that can only come from you when things are bad just as I do when things are good. You are a good father no matter what. Lord help me, like Paul, to learn to be content in all circumstances. Lord, may the things wrong in the world draw me to you and not away from you. In the name of Jesus. Amen.

23

Lions and Dachshunds, Dried Tears, and Eternal Joy

This is the evil in everything that happens under the sun: The same destiny overtakes all. The hearts of people, moreover, are full of evil and there is madness in their hearts while they live, and afterward they join the dead. Anyone who is among the living has hope—even a live dog is better off than a dead lion!

~Ecclesiastes 9:3–4 NIV

Here's something else I've seen on this earth. Races aren't always won by those who run fast. Battles aren't always won by those who are strong. Wise people don't always have plenty of food. Clever people aren't always wealthy. Those who have learned a lot aren't always successful. God controls the timing of every event. He also controls how things turn out. No one knows when trouble will come to them. Fish are caught in nets. Birds are taken in traps. And people are trapped by hard times that come when they don't expect them.

~Ecclesiastes 9: 11–12 NIVR

Then you will be children of your Father who is in heaven. He causes his sun to shine on evil people and good people. He

sends rain on those who do right and those who don't.
~Matthew 5:45 NIVR

But now that he is dead, why should I go on fasting? Can I bring him back again? I will go to him, but he will not return to me."
~2 Samuel 12:23 NIV

He will swallow up death forever. The Lord and King will wipe away the tears from everyone's face. He will remove the shame of his people from the whole earth. The Lord has spoken.
~Isaiah 25:8 NIVR

"This is the final perfection of the soul: to be so grounded in the love of God as to be able to respond with faithful obedience when all joy is absent, and no favorable consequences are foreseen as flowing from the suffering."
~Marilyn McCord Adams

"Love of God is pure when joy and suffering inspire an equal degree of gratitude."
~Simone Weil

March 27th, 2023, I dropped my nine-year-old off at the school bus stop in the morning. I told him to "make today your masterpiece" and that I loved him.... like I do every day. Later that afternoon I picked my son up from school at 3:30 like I always do. I am so grateful for that because that morning in Nashville three other parents got their nine-year-old children ready and off to school, just like they always did... but they were not able to pick their child up after school. Their children were lost due to a school shooting. Those children were taken from their parents, from us.

I have hopes, dreams, and visions of the future for my

nine-year-old just like I am sure these parents did. I still have these hopes and dreams for my son, but these parents have lost the hopes and dreams they had for their kids, and that is just beyond sad.

It's been said by many from Tolkien to Guirgis, "No parent should have to bury their child."

A parent burying a child is unnatural even for the normal natural evils we have to face. But to add that these children's lives were taken by a person's abuse of the gift of free will given by God to us humans makes it even worse. It isn't right, it isn't fair. It is evidence that this world is fallen and not as it should be.

Life truly and utterly is not fair. Because the world is fallen there are natural evils which through no direct fault of our own happen to us. There are the moral evil choices of other humans whose consequences through no direct fault of our own happen to us. Then there are even our own morally evil choices and the consequences of them that affect us, no matter how sorry we are that we made the choice. All of this feels so random, so unfair. Little girls get raped; puppies die. Even typing those words lets me know something is off. It feels gross to even type those words much less that they are a part of the world we live in. Eventually suffering is one thing all of us have in common. Happiness is not always doled out in equal amounts; the amount of suffering is for sure not always distributed evenly, but the inevitability that we will all experience suffering is. Death comes for all. Yet as long as we have breath there is hope. A live dachshund (all twenty pounds of it) is infinitely more powerful than a dead lion (all 500 pounds of him). Why? Because he is alive. For believers this is not just life in the physical sense but in the reality of eternity.

So, there is still hope. There is always hope because there is the promise of eternal salvation in Jesus. Who wins and who loses in life feels random, yet God is sovereign even when a disturbed individual chooses to end the lives of innocent children. Free will is a gift from God that he can't always interfere with if free will is to be truly free.

Humans are free to choose evil, and God is in control. It sure does not seem that way when there are things like school shootings, but God doesn't have to command our choices nor build contingencies for them. He has them under control while not controlling them. That is a hard sentence to type even though I know it is philosophically and theologically true. Our experience of life can be so random, and hard times come to us when we don't expect them to; we lose jobs, we get cancer, we lose loved ones, our kids' rebel, school children and those who care for them lose their lives.

We can only experience these things as senseless apart from God. We don't know when trouble will come. We aren't in a position to predict when or understand why, but God is. We may not feel like we deserve some of the evils that come our way (and we might be right in a sense), and we know children don't deserve to lose their lives. We also can't say we earned the right to our salvation either. None of us can be righteous enough to cast the first stone or earn our way to God. So yes, life truly isn't fair—in fact it is hard as hell sometimes. Life can be dark, sad and tragic, but there is more good than bad which is why the bad sticks out like it does. We have a God who loves us enough to give us free will, to use even the most senseless tragedies to drive us toward him and who sent his son to die for all of us. Life isn't fair, and thank God it isn't. Once we are so attached to Jesus that he is all we see, then whether we suffer or prosper we can be content in all circumstances, even in the saddest. Friends, we should cry our tears (Jesus did) and feel the grief when this fallen world proves itself fallen again and again and yet be content in the hope that all things will be made new in Jesus Christ. Death is not the end for those who believe. For those who believe they will scoop up those children and hold them in their arms again as they are both held in the arms of Jesus. Then the tears of today will be forgotten is the vastness of eternity.

Father, teach me to keep my eyes on Jesus. Always and only on Jesus. Whether suffering from something someone did to me, I did to myself, or just something random, keep the eyes of my heart only on Jesus. Fill my heart with gratitude and contentment because no matter how I suffer and how much I lose physically, mentally, emotionally, I cannot lose spiritually because I have you, Jesus. Lord, even when the loss and pain are so vile, so off, so overwhelming may I see you through rivers of tears. Help me grieve and be sad but also rejoice in that I have your salvation so therefore I can have your joy. Let me consider it pure joy to suffer for you and in the same ways you did. In Jesus name. Amen

24

Hold Me

"So be quiet and let me speak. Then I won't care what happens to me. Why do I put myself in danger? Why do I take my life in my hands? Even if God kills me, I'll still put my hope in him. I'll argue my case in front of him. No matter how things turn out, I'm sure I'll still be saved. After all, no ungodly person would dare to come into his court."

~Job 13: 13–16 NIV

"I am certain that I never did grow in grace one half so much anywhere as I have upon the bed of pain."

~Charles Spurgeon

"The two-year-old heart patient is convinced of its mother's love, not by her cognitively inaccessible reasons, but by her intimate care and presence through its painful experience."

~Marilyn McCord-Adams

Just because there does not appear to be a reason for suffering does mean there is no reason for suffering. When I got my first car, the gas gage did not work properly. The gage did not read accurately after it passed a half a tank. I would have to fill up at the beginning of the week (Monday). I knew for a normal week I would not have to fill up again until the following Monday. I knew that driving around town to places I normally drove, such as school and work, I could reasonably assume the car would not run out of gas. I did not however actually know for certain at any time how much gas was in the tank after it passed a half a tank (between half a tank and empty the gage did not work). Now if I drove to the town an hour away on Friday night to see my girlfriend, was I in a reasonable position to assume I had enough gas to make it to next Monday just because the gage was not on empty? Keep in mind on the one hand cars get better mileage on the highway than in town, but I was adding an additional 100 miles to my normal usage. Now if the tank read a quarter of a tank it would appear to me that I still had some gas. I also would not normally have to fill up between Mondays, but I had used the car in a "gratuitous" manner, so would I be in a reasonable position to know whether I needed to fill up or not? I would say the amount of gas left in the tank was not accessible to me and therefore my seeability was such that I could not trust what appeared to be true, either by data or inference from the past. My ignorance of the situation does not mean there is not gas in the tank, ignorance does not mean something has no meaning.

Friends we often hear of others and perhaps have even ourselves accused God of not existing or being mean because things are not perfect or the amount of evil in the world seems too much, too "gratuitous." We don't live in a world where every day is rainbows and unicorns or steaks and super bowls. Life is hard, real hard sometimes. But perhaps it is God's mercy and wisdom that allows these evils. Even though these evils may seem senseless, extreme, gratuitous, or even cruel to us who only see in part and know in part. How do humans grow in courage? Something to fear is a necessary condition to developing courage. How do humans develop empathy? By either suffering ourselves or the suffering of others, most times both.

Humans, like a pearl in an oyster shell, develop character and virtue from the pain caused by the irritant of sand.

A child will not understand the pain of the surgeon's scalpel nor why his father allowed the surgeon to hurt her. The father knows the pain is for the ultimate good of fixing a heart issue. The child cannot understand why but even if it could be explained to the child that would not take away the pain of the experience or make it hurt any less. What the child needs is the loving embrace of her father not an explanation. Most children run to the parent when pain and suffering come. God the father might allow a lack of goodness (pain and suffering) in part, so that there may be an increase of goodness in the whole. The suffering needs to occur to fix the heart issue and to cause the child to run into the embrace of the father. Friends, the good parent does not maximize pleasure, but does maximize good. God is a good maximizer, not a pleasure maximizer.

Ultimately Job's discourse in chapter 13 and where he ends up by the end of his story is very analogous with Jesus in the garden who said "not my will but yours be done" or if I may something like this:

Young daughter: That needle is going to hurt, Daddy, why are you going to let that man stick that needle in me.

Father: Because, baby girl, it will help make you sleep so the doctor can make you all better.

Young daughter: So he has to hurt me to make me better? I don't understand.

Father: I know, sweet girl, but Daddy has you.

Young daughter: "Okay, Daddy. Will you hold me?

Father: "Of course baby. I've got you.

Friends, ultimately Job's answer to suffering he didn't deserve was surrender. Jesus' answer to the suffering he was about to go through that he for sure didn't deserve was surrender. What we need to learn from the lessons in the pain of suffering is to surrender and to ask our Daddy to hold us.

Father, Abba, Daddy, Jesus... hold me. Amen

25

The Gift of Choice

So, God let them go. He allowed them to do what their sinful hearts wanted to. He let them commit sexual sins. They made one another's bodies impure by what they did. They chose a lie instead of the truth about God. They worshiped and served created things. They didn't worship the Creator. But he is praised forever. Amen.

~Romans 1:24–25 NIV

"He [God] can't give these creatures the freedom to perform evil and at the same time prevent them from doing so."

~Alvin Plantinga

"Man has free choice, or otherwise counsels, exhortations, commands, prohibitions, rewards, and punishments would be in vain."

~Augustine

Paul states, "they chose" and "He allowed." One of the greatest gifts God gives humans is the free will to choose. Part of that gift though is the ability to choose wrong. This is where moral evil comes into play. Moral evil is the evil that arises out of the acts or intentions of agents who have free will. In other words, moral evil is the result of what humans choose.

God cannot grant humans libertarian choice (free will) and yet intervene or prevent humans from making wrong choices. If the choice is between A and B, but every time B is chosen, it becomes A, then B is never truly an option, and thus it is a faux choice. Humans must have the ability to choose wrong in order for humanity to maintain its status as morally free beings. If God intervened at all points of evil/moral choices, man would cease to be free and cease to be a morally capable being. Freedom of choice necessitates the possibility of evil. Eventually humans will always choose evil, and God cannot both grant the freedom of free will and prevent that free will from choosing evil. He allows our sinful hearts to do what we want; that is a part of the gift of free will.

We are also free to respond to his calling and love him. Friends, we are free to choose to align our choices with his will and to choose righteousness. We are free to worship and praise the creator forever.

Father in heaven, thank you for the gift of free will. Thank you for allowing me to have choices. You did not have to create me with that freedom, and I thank you for doing so. Lord help me day by day to choose to worship you, Creator, and not created things. Holy Spirit guide my choices towards righteousness and away from evil. Jesus thank you for dying on the cross for me because we both know I will inevitably fail and will choose evil. When I do fail, Holy Spirit convict me quickly to repentance. Thank you, Jesus, for the reconciliation of the cross and the grace it affords me. Help me to be ever grateful for it and never abuse it. In the name of Jesus. Amen.

26

Foggy Mirrors and Analogies

Now we see only a dim likeness of things. It is as if we were seeing them in a foggy mirror. But someday we will see clearly. We will see face to face. What I know now is not complete. But someday I will know completely, just as God knows me completely.

~1 Corinthians 13:12 NIV

How very rich are God's wisdom and knowledge! How he judges is more than we can understand! The way he deals with people is more than we can know! "Who can ever know what the Lord is thinking? Or who can ever give him advice?" (Isaiah 40:13) "Has anyone ever given anything to God, so that God has to pay them back?" (Job 41:11) All things come from him. All things are directed by him. All things are for his praise.
May God be given the glory forever! Amen.

~Romans 11:33–36 NIV

"It seems that no word is applied literally to God… No word can be said literally of something if it is more truly denied of it than predicated of it. But all such words as 'good,' 'wise,' and the like are more truly denied of God

than predicated of him… Therefore, none of these names belong to God in their literal sense."

~Thomas Aquinas

"Thus the sun which possesses light perfectly, can shine by itself; whereas the moon which has the nature of light imperfectly, sheds only a borrowed light."

~Thomas Aquinas

Aquinas asserts that humans speak and know about God by analogy. The human understanding of God as omnipotent, omniscient, wholly good is neither the exact same nor completely different from what/whom God actually is in totality. God's goodness and God as the center and circumference of good are more unlike human good and goodness than the same (literal). The human conception of God is a gesture towards or a shadow of God's power, knowledge, and state of good, but it is neither utterly unrelated nor precisely the same. Like the guy playing the cover of "Free Bird" can't play it the same as Lynyrd Skynyrd—even if he is playing all the right notes at the correct tempo, it is still a cover. It is an analogy of the original. Analogies always break down.

Human understanding of God, an omnipotent, omniscience, and wholly good essence, is more dissimilar to who God really is than they are like how God really is, even though each of those attributes are true. It's not that God is good, but that God IS good. God is not made up of attributes of goodness, but God is goodness. God is simple. Because of this, humans must remain humble. When we say an omnipotent, omniscient, wholly good God would not allow this much suffering, we are by our own definition of God not in a position to know or understand what an omnipotent, omniscient, wholly good would do because we are none of those things. Our own definition demands we won't understand what God would or would not do.

A foggy mirror shows you an image, and there is accuracy in that image to an extent, but there are also distortions. Aquinas calls this analogy; Paul calls it seeing in part and knowing in part. God is more than we can understand.

Aquinas speaks of shades of likeness and the analogy of being. Friends, when we define God (which is already a reduction because a human mind could never define God accurately) as omnipotent, omniscient, wholly good we are admitting we could never give God advice or judge what God would do. All we can do is remain humble knowing all things come from him, all things are directed by him, all things are for his praise. To him be the glory forever!

Father God, you are beyond me. You made me in your likeness, but you are the prototype. I can, and will, never fully understand you until the day I meet you face to face. Forgive me for the times I demand or expect you to fit into my understanding. Forgive me for expecting that I, a sinner, finite and frail would understand you, who are immutable, absolute eternal, divinely simple, and beyond my understanding of omnipotent, omniscient, wholly good. Forgive me for trying to get you to fit into what I think you would and should do. I am too bold, and I have sinned, forgive me. Thank you for giving me shades of likeness for understanding you—in relationships, in nature, in art. Thank you for your word which gives me all the understanding I need to live a life for you and wholly surrendered to you. In Jesus name. Amen.

27

Do I Have to Understand to Find Meaning?

You don't know the path the wind takes.
You don't know how a baby is made inside its mother.
So you can't understand how God works either.
He made everything.

~Ecclesiastes 11:5 NIVR

Everything has now been heard.
And here's the final thing I want to say.
Have respect for God and obey his commandments.
This is what he expects of all human beings.
God will judge everything people do.
That includes everything they try to hide.
He'll judge everything, whether it's good or evil.

~Ecclesiastes 12:13–14 NIVR

"God is too good to be unkind, and He is too wise to be mistaken. And when we cannot trace His hand, we must trust His heart."

~Charles Spurgeon

"God can't give us peace and happiness apart from himself

because there is no such thing."

~C.S. Lewis

In an earlier devotion I used the example of my gas gage to show how things are not as they always appear to be. This analogy showed a likeness between two situations (that is what analogies do). Analogies are meant to show correspondence, but that correspondence is always limited. I used the analogy of the broken gas tank in my car to illustrate humanity's epistemic situation when it comes to reasons why God would allow seemingly pointless evil. While it worked to show that I probably would have a hard time knowing how much gas was in the tank given the extra use, I could have easily found out. I could have researched that the tank in my car was a fifteen-gallon tank and that in the city my car got twenty-four miles to the gallon while it got twenty-eight miles to the gallon on the highway. I could have reset the trip setting on the odometer and by simple math gained reasonable epistemic access to whether my car would run out of gas or not. The analogy breaks down.

The same is true of our understanding of God. While we are made in his likeness, and we have his word to guide us to a real knowledge of God, the analogy will break down. The correspondence is limited. I truly wish we could understand why all of the evil in the world happens. I wish I knew why evil had to exist at all. I wish that even if evil did have to exist that the amount of evil could be greatly reduced. But my wishing this does not make it any less likely that there is a God, and that God has reasons for allowing such evil. I can't understand how God works. That isn't a satisfying answer in one sense but in another it is. I can't understand why, but that means I don't have to carry the burden of knowing. In Ecclesiastes Solomon walks us through his journey of literally trying everything that life has to offer to find meaning—sex (with as many women as he could), achievement, wealth, drink, food, parties, military strength, even knowledge—but nothing gave any meaning. Finding the answers at the end to all of these paths led Solomon to declare them meaningless. Just because I cannot understand why God allows suffering doesn't mean God does not have a reason. It also does not mean that God is a bully picking on humanity. In fact, the reason evil stands out so starkly and offends us so deeply is that there is far more good in existence, in creation, in life than there is evil. If hurricanes were a daily occurrence, they would not seem so evil. If kindness were rarer and meanness more common, being mean would not seem so… well, mean. The shock is not the amount of evil in the world but rather the amount of good. Friends, evil stands out because it stands in contrast to good. In this world there is far more love than there is hate. Which makes sense since God IS love.

Friends the best understanding of and response to the problem of evil is:

1. We can never and therefore aren't responsible for understanding why God allows evil and the amount he allows, but we can know that God's heart is good.
2. Evil will not go unjudged.
3. God allows/brings about far more good than evil.
4. There either is no meaning to life or meaning can only be found in doing the will of God. Peace cannot be found where meaning cannot be found.
5. The best thing we can do is love the Lord with all our heart and follow his commands.

Father God, you are the author of existence itself. You hold meaning in your hands. Life has meaning only in you and only because of you. Lord, I do not understand why you allow the evil you do. Help me to trust that you have your reasons… even when I am the one suffering. Even when those I love are suffering. Lord, thank you for being a merciful judge. Father, thank you for sending Jesus to take away the evil that I do. Thank you, Jesus, for submitting yourself to the cross to redeem and erase the evil that I have done, and evil I will do. Help me to do what you expect of me, to love you with all my heart and to love my neighbor as myself. That is where meaning in my life is found... in doing your will... in loving you and in loving others. In the name of Jesus. Amen.

28

Lord, hear my prayer. Listen to my cry for help.
Don't turn your face away from me when I'm in trouble.
Pay attention to me. When I call out for help, answer me
quickly.

~Psalm 102: 1–2 NIV

A person can do nothing better than to eat and drink and
find satisfaction in their own toil. This too, I see, is from the
hand of God, for without him, who can eat or find enjoyment?
To the person who pleases him, God gives wisdom, knowledge
and happiness, but to the sinner he gives the task of gathering
and storing up wealth to hand it over to the one who pleases
God. This too is meaningless, a chasing after the wind.

~Ecclesiastes 2:24–26 NIV

For to me, to live is Christ and to die is gain.

~Philippians 1:21 NIV

I'm not saying this because I need anything. I have learned to
be content no matter what happens to me. I know what it's like
not to have what I need. I also know what it's like to have more

95

than I need. I have learned the secret of being content no matter what happens. I am content whether I am well fed or hungry. I am content whether I have more than enough or not enough. I can do all this by the power of Christ. He gives me strength.
~Philippians 4:11–13 NIVR

"Final and perfect happiness cannot consist in anything other the vision of the divine essence."
~Thomas Aquinas

"Misfortunes leave wounds which bleed drop by drop even in sleep; thus, little by little they train man by force and dispose him to wisdom in spite of himself. Man must learn to think of himself as a limited and dependent being and only suffering teaches him this."
~Simone Weil

In *Summa Theologiae* Thomas Aquinas asserts that it is impossible for any created good to constitute man's happiness. For happiness is the perfect good. This is to be found, not in any other person, not in a career, not in health but in God alone because everything else has whatever is good about it by its participation in God's creation. God alone can satisfy us. So perhaps the greatest good and reason for suffering is that it drives us to God? Is losing some lesser good and suffering for it not worth all that it costs us if the loss of that created good drives us toward the ultimate good which can only be found in the arms of Jesus? There is no satisfaction anywhere else. If the usefulness of suffering drives us to Christ it is our gain to suffer.

Father, thank you for the gift of pain and suffering. Let it drive me further and closer to you always. May the pain of this mortal life cause me to long for eternity with you. May the sadness of today cause to me deeply desire being permanently united with you, and may it stir me to tell others of your love and salvation. Lord, comfort me amid suffering, I need you and will need you even more as the inevitability of the end of this life becomes a closer and closer reality both for me and those I love. Lord, help me to live for you through the toils of this life until I gain eternity with you forever. In Jesus name. Amen

Part 4

29

Aren't all Religions Basically the Same?

Salvation is found in no one else, for there is no other name under heaven given to mankind by which we must be saved.

~Acts 4:12 NIV

Whoever has the Son has life; whoever does not have the Son of God does not have life.

~1 John 5:12 NIV

"If Christianity is untrue, then no honest man will want to believe it, however helpful it might be: if it is true, every honest man will want to believe it, even if it gives him no help at all."

~C.S. Lewis

"If Christians are right about Jesus being God, then Muslims and Jews fail in a serious way to love God as God really is, but if Muslims and Jews are right that Jesus is not God but rather a teacher or prophet, then Christians fail in a serious way to love God as God really is."

~Tim Keller

Aren't all religions basically the same? Friends this is a very complex questions because of course there are elements of commonality amongst almost all religions such as the belief in something beyond the physical, beyond humanity and humanity's need to and longing for knowing this reality. The question is complex, but the answer is simple... NO.

All religions aren't basically the same. In fact, the three most influential religions in the world make very exclusive claims. In simple terms they don't teach that other religions lead to salvation. Judaism, Islam, and Christianity share some common beliefs but at their core they do not and cannot (if they want to remain true to the sacred teachings of their religions) accept that the other two lead to the same place their religion does. All three of the most influential monotheistic religions in the world are exclusivist in belief. Contemporary views of exclusivism indict the belief as having too particular a path to God, too particular of an ethical creed, too particular a salvation. In this regard, Islam, Judaism, and Christianity are all guilty. However, just because they are guilty of being exclusivist religions does not make them wrong.

All three view salvation very differently. In Islam salvation is a matter of ascetic ascent and never certain. Judaism teaches that salvation is achieved through good works, prayers, and the justice of God. Friends, Christianity teaches that salvation is by grace alone through the death and resurrection of Jesus.

In Christianity salvation cannot be earned. The faithful Muslim cannot believe Christians will find their way to Allah. The faithful Jew must believe that Christians are following a false Messiah. And yes, that means Christians must believe that salvation is in no one else and that he who does notbelieve in Jesus alone as the Son of God does not have life. Believing otherwise contradicts the words of Jesus, the very one we depend on for the words of life.

Father, thank you for your salvation, thank you for providing a way to be in eternal union with you. Father, help me to be faithful and urgent in my sharing of your gospel so that none may perish. Lord, thank you for your wisdom, justice, and sovereignty. Salvation is found in you alone. In Jesus name. Amen.

30

What is Particularly Particular About Christianity?

For it is by grace you have been saved through faith, and this is not from yourselves; it is the gift of God, not by works, so that no one can boast.

~Ephesians 2:8–9 NIV

"In the Christian understanding, Jesus does not tell us how to live so that we can merit salvation. Rather, he comes to forgive and save us through his life and death in our place. God's grace does not come to people who morally outperform others, but to those who admit their failure to perform and who acknowledge their need for a savior."

~Tim Keller

We believe in one God, the Father almighty, maker of heaven and earth, of all things visible and invisible. And in one Lord Jesus Christ, the only Son of God, begotten from the Father before all ages, God from God, Light from Light, true God from true God, begotten, not made: of the same essence as the Father. Through him all things were made. For us and for our salvation he came down from heaven; he became incarnate by the Holy Spirit and the virgin Mary and was made human. He was crucified for us under Pontius Pilate; he suffered and was buried. The third day he rose again, according to the Scriptures. He ascended to heaven and is seated at the right hand of the Father. He will come again with glory to judge the living and the dead. His kingdom will never end. And we believe in the Holy Spirit, the Lord, the giver of life. He proceeds from the Father, and with the Father and the Son is worshiped and glorified. He spoke through the prophets. We believe in one holy catholic and apostolic church. We affirm one baptism for the forgiveness of sins. We look forward to the resurrection of the dead, and to life in the world to come. Amen.

~The Nicene Creed

You don't have to be a Christian to know that Christians assert that we are saved by faith, but faith in what exactly and what makes Christian faith different than any other faith? What is particularly particular about it? Firstly, Christians believe no human can save themselves. Salvation in Christianity cannot be earned. Salvation is a gift. Second humans must acknowledge that we are in need of a savior. It is not enough to accept the gift if we are not aware of our need for the gift. It is not a passing nonchalant laissez-faire need but a desperate realization of a need that exceeds all other needs by an infinite amount. Salvation in Christianity requires that humans acknowledge the need for a savior as the great singular need of our existence.

So far so good, we know that to be a Christian a person must have faith that salvation comes through faith and that salvation is a gift humans need more than anything else. Thirdly, that salvation is achieved through Jesus. Jesus is the savior. So, Christianity is faith that salvation comes through Jesus as a gift that humans need more than anything else, and humans must acknowledge the need for that gift. Everything we have said so far is 100% true in Christianity and must be believed for salvation. Unfortunately this is where most people stop. This is where cultural Christianity stops. This is where good old boy, Bible belt thumpin', mom and apple pie, baseball and shotgun American Christianity stops. But this does not go far enough, it does not get us to understand what we need to believe about Jesus that provides our salvation. Jesus made claims, bold claims, and his followers made bold claims about him. Jesus was not a good old boy any more than he was a social justice warrior (in some ways he was neither and in other ways he was both). Jesus was so much more. There are very particular things that must be believed about this Jesus who offers the gift of salvation that all humans need. Luckily for us these beliefs where codified by early church fathers at the First Council of Nicaea in 325 AD. This is the concise core articulation of Christianity and the beliefs about Jesus that must be held for someone to receive the gift of salvation from Jesus. These few sentences outline the core tenets of Christianity. The doctrinal statements within the creed outline what is particularly particular about the gift of salvation that humans so desperately need. The creed shows that while the gift is free to humans it was not free to God. Salvation in Christianity is a one-sided freeness. Friends, salvation came at a great sacrifice to God and should not be treated with nonchalant laissez-faire adherence to what it means to have faith in Jesus. Rather, it should inspire a strict deep posture of equal parts reverence to and exuberant joy from the doctrines that outline what it means to have faith in Jesus. Not because the doctrines bring us salvation, but because they show why salvation is free to us and why we need it so desperately.

Father, thank you that salvation is a free gift. Help me to never confuse the matter and think that I am earning my salvation in anything I have or will ever do. I acknowledge I have been saved by grace alone and may I never boast otherwise. While this grace was free to me Lord, I acknowledge it was not free to you. This gift of salvation took you sending your son to earth, to become human. To be born of a human mother, the blessed Mary who was blessed among all women. The gift of salvation came through Jesus, God in the flesh, living a sinless life and then dying a gruesome death on a cross and then being buried. Lord Jesus, you, however, conquered death by rising from the grave on the third day and took your rightful place as God from God to sit at the Father's right hand. Lord Jesus, I acknowledge all this and that you are coming back again to judge all who have, do, and will ever live. Unlike earthly kingdoms Lord Jesus, yours will be eternal.

Holy Spirit you are the giver of life who proceeds from and with the father I worship you and glorify you. You spoke through the prophets, and you still speak through your church today, you even speak to and from me. Give me ears and a heart to hear your voice and to discern it from my own. Lord, I affirm you desire one unified body of believers. Lord, help me be a bonding agent between bodies of believers. May your church be one. Lord, there is one baptism for the forgiveness of sins, thank you for the gift of baptism. Lord, you rose from the dead, not metaphorically but physically rose from the dead, and I believe someday all believers will rise bodily from the dead and be united with you for eternity. In the holy name of Jesus. Amen!

31

He Himself is the Way

My Father's house has many rooms; if that were not so, would I have told you that I am going there to prepare a place for you? And if I go and prepare a place for you, I will come back and take you to be with me that you also may be where I am. You know the way to the place where I am going." Thomas said to him, "Lord, we don't know where you are going, so how can we know the way?" Jesus answered, "I am the way and the truth and the life. No one comes to the Father except through me.
~John 14:2–6 NIV

"If, then, you are looking for the way by which you should go, take Christ, because He Himself is the way."
~Thomas Aquinas

"If you believe what you like in the gospels and reject what you don't like, it is not the gospel you believe but yourself."
~Augustine of Hippo

In this passage Jesus says a lot. He begins by speaking of having to go away, but he is doing so with the promise that he will return. Whether heaven has physical rooms or Jesus was speaking metaphorically here is unknown, but we can know that Jesus is going to the Father to prepare for those who believe in him to be with Jesus and the Father. Ever questioning Thomas asks Jesus how we get to the place that Jesus is preparing. Jesus answers that he is the path to that place. Jesus not only states that he is the path to that place, but he is the manifestation of ultimate reality. Jesus is not claiming to be telling the truth of the situation or even that He is a truth but that he is THE truth. Jesus is saying that he is translucent truth. He is truth from every angle, he is the whole truth. Finally, in answering Thomas, Jesus is stating that he is the very source of eternal life. He is making very metaphysical claims.

1. There is eternal life.
2. That he (Jesus) is the exclusive way to eternal life.

This verse does not say "I one of many ways, a certain kind of truth that might align with "your truth," a good path to eternal life." Jesus is making a very particular claim. He says "no one" and "except." In the contemporary culture of extreme individualism that we live in, narrowness in general makes our heartrate go up. But just because Jesus' answer to Thomas makes contemporary ears uncomfortable does not mean Jesus' words can be ignored. Jesus' claim is not that he is teaching a good set of guidelines or values that if followed will lead to enlightenment and therefore eternal life. No, he is stating here that he himself *is* eternal life.

Friends, Christianity is exclusive at its core. If your Christianity includes the possibility of another religion or any religion other than Christianity as a path to eternal life, then your Christianity is not very Christian. Christianity does not allow for multiple paths to God. Jesus excluded any other way to God the Father and eternal life. If you reject Jesus as the only way to God and eternal life, then you are rejecting Christianity.

Stated as logical proposition Jesus' claims here are as follows:

P1: If anyone comes to the Father, then one comes through Jesus.

2: One does not come through Jesus.

So, one does not come to the Father. [valid by modus tollens]
P2: One comes to the Father.
So, one comes through Jesus. [valid by modus ponens]

Friends, Jesus eliminates any notion of universalism with those who do not accept him as savior. Jesus demands all or nothing. He is either the son of God or he is not, there is no other way to assess his exclusive claims. For those who take Jesus' claims to be true, remember in this same passage he also promises to come back for us so that we can live and have relationship with him for all eternity, and that is truly good news.

Jesus, you are the one true God. You Jesus yourself are the way, the truth, and the life. I believe you are my life and my salvation. I have access to the Father only in your death and resurrection. I love you Jesus, thank you for first loving me and drawing me to you. Amen

32

The Tender Shepherd Who Keeps the Wolves Away

"A thief comes only to steal and kill and destroy. I have come so they may have life. I want them to have it in the fullest possible way.

"I am the good shepherd. The good shepherd gives his life for the sheep. The hired man is not the shepherd and does not own the sheep. So when the hired man sees the wolf coming, he leaves the sheep and runs away. Then the wolf attacks the flock and scatters it. The man runs away because he is a hired man. He does not care about the sheep.

"I am the good shepherd. I know my sheep, and my sheep know me. They know me just as the Father knows me and I know the Father. And I give my life for the sheep.

"I have other sheep that do not belong to this sheep pen. I must bring them in too. They also will listen to my voice. Then there will be one flock and one shepherd. The reason my Father loves me is that I give up my life. But I will take it back again."
~John 10:10–17 NIVR

"Pagan philosophers Plato and Aristotle arrived through human reasoning at the existence of God, speaking of him in vague, impersonal terms as the Uncaused Cause and the

110

Immovable Mover. The prophets of Israel had revealed the God of Abraham, Isaac, and Jacob in a more intimate and passionate manner. But only Jesus revealed that God is a Father of incomparable tenderness…"

~Brennan Manning

"Since the day that Jesus first appeared on the scene, we have developed vast theological systems, organized world-wide churches, filled libraries with brilliant christological scholarship, engaged in earthshaking controversies, and embarked on crusades, reforms, and renewals. Yet there are still precious few of us with sufficient folly to make the mad exchange of everything for Christ; only a remnant with the confidence to risk everything on the gospel of grace; only a minority who stagger about with the delirious joy of the man who found the buried treasure."

~Brennan Manning

The world has over four thousand religions ranging from Hinduism, Buddhism, Taoism to Jedism (worshiping the force). Christianity and Islam are the two largest religions in the world. Both are Abrahamic religions along with Judaism. Abrahamic religions have historically had and presently maintain the most prominent influence upon humanity. All three religions are ortho-doxically exclusivist and view pluralism in essence as evil or heretical. In plain terms Judaism, Islam, and Christianity believe they are correct, and to varying but necessary degrees the others are wrong. One way Christianity is distinct from the other two major religions is the way Christianity views how a person can receive salvation. In Islam soteriologically speaking salvation is a matter of ascetic ascent and never certain. In other words, a person must live a good moral life according to religious beliefs, but a person can never be sure of their salvation. Judaism is a nationalistic religion in that salvation is found in both the practice of living in adherence to the law but also identifying as a member of God's chosen people (whether by ethnicity, national citizenship, or being a Judaist.) In Islam and Judaism, salvation at least partially depends on the work and diligence of the follower.

In Christianity, salvation cannot be earned but is a gift from God, the contrast in beliefs about salvation between these religions are incompatible as a gift is either free or it is not. It is not a gift if a friend wants to take me to dinner as a birthday present but wants me to pay for the dessert. Salvation is either earned or it is a gift. Jesus says that he did not come to burden life but to give life. Jesus says that he will defend those who follow him even unto death. In contrast to the savior Judaism expected and way of salvation it taught, Jesus said he has "other sheep that do not belong to this sheep pen." Jesus eliminates a nationalistic view of salvation (take note America). Jesus didn't even say he *wanted* to bring others in but that he *must* bring these other sheep in. Jesus gave up his life so that salvation can be a gift freely given to all who call upon his name for salvation. In Jesus we find a tender shepherd who cares for his sheep. The buried treasure of salvation in Christianity is grace. Christianity is exclusive, but exclusively a religion where the founder consistently said not to be afraid to be people who were used to being afraid.

Friends, Christianity is a religion exclusively where a middle eastern first-century man claimed to be God yet did not seek power or gain but rather gave up his life willingly so that those who accept him might be reconciled to the Father. In Christianity there is nothing we can do to earn our salvation; it is the free gift of the tender shepherd who cares for his sheep.

Father, thank you for the Son, thank you for sending your Son, and thank you for pouring your wrath out on him and not on me. Lord Jesus, thank you for being a savior who not only participated in our suffering but took it on when you did not have to and did not deserve to suffer for me. Jesus, thank you for the free gift of salvation. Lord, thank you that I could never earn it for I might be tempted to think I am worthy to be saved. Always keep fresh in my mind that I am worthy to be saved but only because of your death and resurrection on the cross. I am worthy of salvation not because of anything I have or ever could do, but I am worthy because you say I am worthy. In the holy name of Jesus. Amen

33

The Miracle of Miracles

Early on the first day of the week, Mary Magdalene went to the tomb. It was still dark. She saw that the stone had been moved away from the entrance. So she ran to Simon Peter and another disciple, the one Jesus loved. She said, "They have taken the Lord out of the tomb! We don't know where they have put him!" So Peter and the other disciple started out for the tomb. Both of them were running. The other disciple ran faster than Peter. He reached the tomb first. He bent over and looked in at the strips of linen lying there. But he did not go in. Then Simon Peter came along behind him. He went straight into the tomb. He saw the strips of linen lying there. He also saw the funeral cloth that had been wrapped around Jesus' head. The cloth was still lying in its place. It was separate from the linen. The disciple who had reached the tomb first also went inside. He saw and believed. They still did not understand from Scripture that Jesus had to rise from the dead.

~John 20:1–9 NIVR

Greater love has no man than this, that a man lay down his life for his friends.

~John 15:13 NIV

If there is no resurrection of the dead, then not even Christ has been raised. And if Christ has not been raised, our preaching is useless and so is your faith. More than that, we are then found to be false witnesses about God, for we have testified about God that he raised Christ from the dead. But he did not raise him if in fact the dead are not raised.

~1 Corinthians 15:13–15 NIV

If only for this life we have hope in Christ, we are of all people most to be pitied.

~1 Corinthians 15:19 NIV

"If Jesus rose from the dead, then you have to accept all that he said; if he didn't rise from the dead, then why worry about any of what he said? The issue on which everything hangs is not whether or not you like his teaching but whether or not he rose from the dead."

~Tim Keller

"The miracle of the resurrection, and the theology of that miracle, comes first."

~C.S. Lewis

The resurrection is the most particular and exclusive claim in history. It not only defies normal logic and science, but it also defies experience. Neither Abraham nor Mohammed claimed to be God, nor did they claim to rise from the dead. Christians themselves concede that if the resurrection did not occur, their faith is false—not partially true—false. Jesus claimed to be God and was raised from the dead. There are some that claim the resurrection was a group hallucination. The problem with this is that Jesus appeared to those who were not looking for him such as Paul and James. Some claim that maybe the

Romans thought Jesus had died but that he in fact was still alive. To this I would argue that the Romans were experts at killing and probably had a pretty good idea of how to diagnose if someone were dead or not. The apostles claimed he appeared to them and most all of them died for that claim. I don't know many people who would die for a conspiracy or a lie. Paul states he appeared to 500 people. Even skeptics admit the disciples believed Jesus appeared to them.

Friends, if Jesus did not physically rise from the dead, not allegorically resurrect, or merely spiritually rise from the dead but physically rise from the dead, then Christians are most to be pitied. But if he did then that means the laws of nature don't have a hold on Jesus, he has hold of them. In the famous C.S. Lewis trilemma (Lord Liar Lunatic) he describes that Jesus is either morally corrupt, mentally ill, or he is who he said he was.

Some say he could be a legend, but that holds no intellectual weight (even from atheist scholars). Orthodox Christian teachings have always held that Jesus literally physically rose from the dead and someday so would his followers. The Nicene Creed states, "For our sake he was crucified under Pontius Pilate, he suffered death and was buried, and rose again on the third day in accordance with the scriptures." Keep in mind the Nicene Creed is a doctrinal statement of what is correct belief in Christianity that dates back to 325 CE. Simply put if Jesus did not rise from the dead throw all of Christianity out, but if Jesus did rise from the dead (which a mountain of evidence points to being the case) then throw everything else but Jesus out.

Father God, thank you for sending your Son to die on the cross for my sins. Jesus, thank you for dying on the cross for me and for conquering death and rising back to life so that I have eternal hope in your salvation, the only salvation that exists. Jesus, you are God, the only way to the Father, and you proved that on the cross and the empty tomb. Praise God the Father, God the son, and God the

Holy Spirit, the three in one who rescued humans from sin and satisfied the Father's justice for all who believe. Amen.

34

One Woman, Three Marys, or a Whole Gaggle

All Scripture is God-breathed and is useful for teaching, rebuking, correcting and training in righteousness.
~2 Timothy 3:16 NIV

After the Sabbath, at dawn on the first day of the week, Mary Magdalene and the other Mary went to look at the tomb.
~Matthew 28:1 NIV

When the Sabbath was over, Mary Magdalene, Mary the mother of James, and Salome bought spices so that they might go to anoint Jesus' body. Very early on the first day of the week, just after sunrise, they were on their way to the tomb
~Mark 16:1–2 NIV

It was Mary Magdalene, Joanna, Mary the mother of James, and the others with them who told this to the apostles.
~Luke 24:10 NIV

"The traditional definition of biblical inerrancy maintains that the Bible is accurate and completely free of error. Inerrancy does not require, however, that the biblical texts be free of any personal perspective or idiosyncrasies. In fact, the existence of these distinctive features only helps us recognize the accounts as true eye-witness statements written by real people who revealed their human gifts (and limitations) along the way. These characteristics can help us have confidence in both the accuracy and the reliability of the accounts."

~J. Warner Wallace

"There are times when an eyewitness gets something wrong. In fact, I've seen this repeatedly over the course of my career. Witnesses are people, and people make mistakes. But the fact that a witness might be wrong about a particular detail or element of the crime does not necessarily disqualify them or render their testimony unreliable. If that were the case, we would never be able to prosecute anyone for anything. When examining the reliability of an eyewitness and encountering some factual error, I've got to determine (1) if the errant aspect of the statement is relevant to the larger issues in the case, and (2) the reason why the witness got the detail wrong in the first place. If a victim of a robbery misidentifies the kind of shirt the suspect wore at the time of the robbery, I have to ask myself if this misidentification makes the victim an unreliable witness."

~J. Warner Wallace

How can there be mistakes if all scripture is God-breathed? How many women went to the tomb? Perhaps Luke (being a very detailed writer) accounted for all the women present, while the other writers only highlighted the important women. But perhaps some of the writers' personal perspectives were factually incorrect. Does this mean there is an error in the Bible? I would say no. They were telling the truth from their subjective eyewitness account, which will always be somewhat different from another's eyewitness account.

Let me give an example. My oldest son (Zeke—lead singer and songwriter for Tooth-N-Nail recording artist Idle Threat) and I went to see Gary Clark Jr. in concert a few summers ago. When we got back from the show and were telling my wife about it we had different recollections on the order of the set list. We both noted that GCJ opened with his song "Bright Lights," but we differed on when he played his cover of the Beatles song "Come Together." We were both telling the subjective truth. Neither of us were lying nor were we delusional. We were telling the absolute truth as it were true to us, but we both could not be objectively correct. Either one or perhaps both of us were incorrect when it came to objective truth.

This is the same with the discrepancies in the gospels (including how many angels were at the empty tomb and exactly what time of day it was.). Each gospel reports the subjective truth of the perspective of the eyewitnesses, but they cannot all be correct when it comes to the objective truth. This is not a mark against the reliability of the gospels but for it. The fact that my son and I remember things slightly different is good evidence that we are both telling the truth. If our perspectives lined up perfectly it would be reasonable to think either one of us was not there at all and was just borrowing the others true perspective or that we got together before hand and determined what the story was going to be. Just because an account is incorrect as far as objective truth does not mean the account is untrue or not reliable. Friends, the Bible is trustworthy, reliable, authoritative, and conveys God's message and character in a sufficient manner for all we need for salvation and being in an obedient relationship with God. Even if we never how exactly how many Marys were at the empty tomb—or whether it is pronounced Sal-o-may or Sal-ah-me like the delicious meat.

Father in heaven, thank you for your word. Thank you for its power and authority for showing me who you are and why I need you so much. Thank you your written word teaches me, transforms me, and challenges me to be a better person. Father, may the words of scripture be ever on my mind and my tongue. Lord give me a thirst to read, memorize, and imprint your words on my heart. Let my first go-to source of knowledge and wisdom always be your word. Thank you, Lord, for the message of salvation and grace weaved throughout the singular story in your word. The love story between you God and humanity, between you Lord and me. In the name of Jesus, I give you all praise and honor. Amen.

35

Jesus was a Momma's Boy

On the third day a wedding took place at Cana in Galilee. Jesus' mother was there, and Jesus and his disciples had also been invited to the wedding. When the wine was gone, Jesus' mother said to him, "They have no more wine." "Woman, why do you involve me?" Jesus replied. "My hour has not yet come." His mother said to the servants, "Do whatever he tells you." Nearby stood six stone water jars, the kind used by the Jews for ceremonial washing, each holding from twenty to thirty gallons. Jesus said to the servants, "Fill the jars with water;" so, they filled them to the brim. Then he told them, "Now draw some out and take it to the master of the banquet." They did so, and the master of the banquet tasted the water that had been turned into wine. He did not realize where it had come from, though the servants who had drawn the water knew. Then he called the bridegroom aside and said, "Everyone brings out the choice wine first and then the cheaper wine after the guests have had too much to drink; but you have saved the best till now." What Jesus did here in Cana of Galilee was the first of the signs through which he revealed his glory; and his disciples believed in him.

~John 2:1–11 NIV

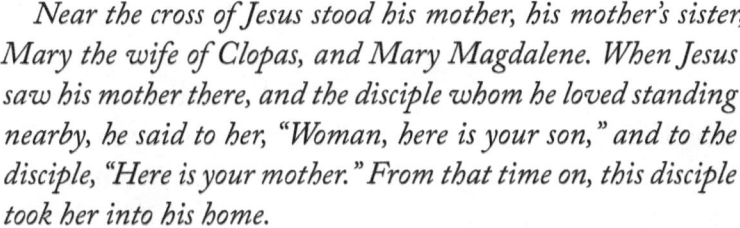

Near the cross of Jesus stood his mother, his mother's sister, Mary the wife of Clopas, and Mary Magdalene. When Jesus saw his mother there, and the disciple whom he loved standing nearby, he said to her, "Woman, here is your son," and to the disciple, "Here is your mother." From that time on, this disciple took her into his home.

~John 19:25–27 NIV

"Jesus repeatedly welcomed women his contemporaries despised."

~Rebecca McLaughlin

"Then that little man in black there, he says women can't have as much rights as men, 'cause Christ wasn't a woman! Where did your Christ come from? Where did Christ come from? From God and a woman! Man had nothing to do with Him."

~Sojourner Truth

Friends, especially to my sisters in Christ, God cares for you. You are fearfully and wonderfully made. God made them male and female. God honors, protects, and respects women. The Bible affirms women and raises them to a status that runs counter to the cultures they existed in. While some passages of the Bible are hard to read and not insert our contemporary subjective selves, it is hard to deny that given the cultures the Bible was written in, contextually the Bible affirms women both in the old and new testaments. There is no better example of how God honors, protects, respects, and serves women in the New Testament then how Jesus interacted with his mother Mary.

But we can also find many examples of God's elevation of women compared to their cultural context in the Old Testament. I am particularly fond of the story Susanna which is found in the Greek

(Septuagint) version of the book of Daniel. In this story, the beautiful woman Susanna is falsely accused and convicted of adultery by Hebrew judges. These judges were the same two men who tried to bully Susanna into having an illicit sexual encounter with the two of them. It was, in fact, Susanna's rejection that motivated the men to make the accusation. As Susanna was being taken to be stoned, she prayed to God, and he heard her prayer. God impressed upon Daniel to investigate further. Daniel did the old *Law and Order* separate the witnesses trick and discovered Susanna to be blameless. I love this story because it shows that God was always concerned with women's rights and was never okay with men bullying their way with women.

Today, friends, I want to focus on two examples of God's care of women found in two interactions between Jesus and his mom; one at the beginning of his ministry and the other at the end of Jesus' life.

If you notice in the first passage when Mary told Jesus the wedding party was out of wine, she did so with the implicit message that Jesus could do something about it. That is why this is Jesus' first public miracle, but it may not have been his first miracle. We see that Mary ignored Jesus saying his time had not come and told the servants to do what Jesus said. She assumed Jesus would do what she was asking without waiting for his answer because, well, she was his mom, and she was asking him to. Jesus did not play the God card with her but rather just honored his mother by doing what she asked. In the second passage at the end of Jesus' life, Jesus was dying on the cross. He was in agonizing pain, but still at the sight of his mother his concern turned toward her. He asked his best friend to make sure to take care of her.

Jesus was as much a momma's boy as there has ever been. Jesus was not the sort of momma's boy that was soft or clingy, but he was a momma's boy in the sense that he was very close with his mother and loved her deeply. His actions show that he honored her, protected her, and respected her. If there was ever anyone on earth who would have been justified to ignore or disrespect any woman (even his mother) it would have been Jesus. Yet, Jesus did not do that. He was concerned for women. He honored them just as God the Father did in the Old Testament.

Friends, the church has been flat out wrong at times in its history in how it treated women. Women are not second-class citizens in the kingdom of heaven. They are the daughters of Abraham and souls Jesus died for on the cross. Jesus loves women every bit as much as he did men. I am not arguing complementarian verse egalitarian but rather affirming women in Christ's identity as the daughters of Abraham and the beloved that Jesus died for: women are co-heirs with Christ (Romans 8:17); friends with God (John 15:15); have been blessed with every spiritual blessing men have been (Ephesians 1:3); and have been made complete in Christ (Colossians 2:10). My sisters in Christ are my siblings not my servants, or better stated, women are no more my servants in Christ than I am theirs. In Christ my wife and my daughter are my sisters not to be subjugated but to be honored, respected, protected, and served.

Father in Heaven, thank you for making humans. Thank for maleness and for femaleness. Thank you for moms, sisters by birth and adoption, wives, friends, colleagues, and sisters in Christ. Thank you, Lord, for the helpers that women are and the uniqueness they bring to your kingdom that men lack. Help me to honor each other both male and female. Help me to value others just as much as Jesus valued each of us. Lord lead us, male and female, to honor, protect, respect, and serve one another In the name of Jesus. Amen.

Part 5

36

The Melody of Life Experience

When times are good, be happy.
But when times are bad, here's something to think about.
God has made bad times.
He has also made good times.
So no one can find out anything about what's ahead for them.
~Ecclesiastes 7:14 NIVR

Trust in the LORD with all your heart and lean not on your own understanding. In all your ways submit to him, and he will make your paths straight.

~Proverbs 3:5–6 NIV

And we know that in all things God works for the good of those who love him, who have been called according to his purpose.

~Romans 8:28 NIV

"True reflection presents me to myself not as idle and inaccessible subjectivity, but as identical with my presence in the world and to others, as I am now realizing it: I am all that I see, I am an intersubjective field, not despite my

body and historical situation, but, on the contrary, by being this body and this situation, and through them, all the rest."
~Maurice Merleau-Ponty

"Define yourself radically as one beloved by God. This is the true self. Every other identity is illusion."
~Brennan Manning

An interval is defined as space between objects, points, or units, especially when making uniform amounts of separation. When specifically applied to music, intervals are the distance in pitch between any two notes. A melody is defined as rhythmically and tonally organized sequence of single tones, related to one another in intervals as to make up a particular phrase or idea. Intervals only become melodies when they are experienced consecutively. Moments of experience in our lives do not and cannot happen separate from the previous moments and the moments yet to come. We don't live and experience life moment to moment but rather moment upon moment. The separate single tones don't make a melody; they must be strung together. This is because we don't just have moments, but memories of moments and notions of what moments may come. Life is connected. Our personhood, our concept of self, is constructed of experiences and hopes. Our experiences are not separate from all our past experiences; we live them as connected moments. Our lives include a consciousness of the past and anticipation of a future that may be. No moment lives isolated and unto itself but is connected to all our other moments just like the notes in a song.

For a melody to be beautiful some of the intervals must be dissonant. A dissonant interval is described as conflicting, clashing, urgent, and tense. The contrast between the dissonant intervals and the consonant intervals is what creates the resolve. The feeling of landing home. Without the dissonance we would not feel the resolve of landing home. It is the tension that draws our attention to the resolve.

The same is true of our lives. We cannot be who we are or become who God intends us to be apart from the hard, bad, ugly times. The beautiful times in our lives are made more beautiful by the hard times. Our attention is set on the beauty because of the juxtaposition against the suffering. We could not find our true selves if the false selves were not allowed to die. The moments of tension and resolution crescendo for the believer into becoming more and more like Christ.

Friends, God is weaving our moments with the end goal of us finding and defining ourselves as one loved by him. I could not be who I am without both the joyful and sorrowful moments of my life. Those intervals are an intrinsic part of the melody of who "I" am.

Father, thank you for both the mountain tops and the valleys. Thank you perhaps most of all for the mundane. There is so much to learn from all. Thank you for being intimately involved in my melody. Thank you for knitting me together in my mother's womb and for using all the intervals of my life both dissonant and consonant to guide me toward you. Help me to trust that you are working all my experiences out for ultimate good. Help me to trust you and lean not on my own understanding when I can't see how a particular experience can be used towards good. I don't know what is ahead, and that can be scary, but help me to trust that I am one who is radically loved by you. In the holy name of Jesus. Amen.

37

The Personal Experience of Being Unconditionally Loved

Come to me, all you who are weary and burdened, and I will give you rest.
> ~Matthew 11:28 NIV

"What do you think? If a man owns a hundred sheep, and one of them wanders away, will he not leave the ninety-nine on the hills and go to look for the one that wandered off?
> ~Matthew 18:12 NIV

"You are beautiful, but you are empty," he went on. "One could not die for you. To be sure, an ordinary passerby would think that my rose looked just like you—the rose that belongs to me.

"But in herself alone she is more important than all the hundreds of you other roses: because it is she that I have watered; because it is she that I have put under the glass globe; because it is she that I have sheltered behind the screen; because it is for her that I have killed the cater-pillars (except the two or three that we saved to become butterflies); because it is she that I have listened to, when she grumbled, or boasted, or even sometimes when she said nothing. Because she is my rose."

~Antoine de Saint-Exupéry

"The sinners to whom Jesus directed His messianic ministry were not those who skipped morning devotions or Sunday church. His ministry was to those whom society considered real sinners. They had done nothing to merit salvation. Yet they opened themselves to the gift that was offered them. On the other hand, the self-righteous placed their trust in the works of the Law and closed their hearts to the message of grace."

~Brennan Manning

In 1991, I was sixteen and wild, rebellious, promiscuous. I was the drummer in a pretty popular band around my hometown. I drove a souped-up street racing car with five-on-the-floor (always under the speed limit, Mom—scout's honor). I had long beautiful blond hair (if I do say so myself) down to the middle of my back. I was thinly built but cut (not hard to do as a teen), despite being shy I could smooth talk my way into and out of most situations. Good grades came easy, teachers liked me despite all the above. Girls came easy. I had the world by the tail, and I was also completely full of myself. I was also incredibly insecure and often depressed. I was not close to my family at the time, which is not completely uncommon for teenagers. I mentioned I was quite successful with girls (as a dad now I would have hated me), but the nameless body count did not fill my void, so I decided to look for a real relationship. I decided to clean up my act and find a good girl.

I found one at the high school I attended. She was cute, got good grades, was polite and a little shy. She did not care about being popular at all. She was also a Christian. I thought I remembered what that was about, believe in Jesus (like that he existed) and be a good person. I set out to win this girl's affections by being a good

132

person. I had a large ditch to dig out of as I and my best friend at the time had quite the negative reputation.

Running concurrent to me trying to win this girl over, I replaced all the wild behavior for thrill seeking. I traded the adrenaline rush of girls and alcohol with doing dangerous and stupid stuff as well as stuff that would scare me. My best friend at the time and I would spend the weekends doing stuff like climbing on the roof of our high school's football stadium which was probably 100 feet from the ground and hanging each other off the edge with only the grip of a hand on a shirt to keep us from falling. We would also explore burned down houses or break into an abandoned tuberculosis hospital. We began conducting seances and playing around with Ouija boards. I was testing limits with my friends and trying to impress this Christian girl.

Every day I was trying to pour on the charm. We were chatting on the phone. I was calling her dad, Sir (he still hated me). I was putting on the full court press, flowers, poetry, all of it. I finally got the word that the Christian girl was not interested in me in any way shape or form. No way, no how, never going to happen. I decided since there was no use trying to be a good person I might as well let loose with some friends that night. After making a horrible moral decision, I knew right then, I was not a good person, I was selfish and prideful. I had let down someone very important to me.

I didn't violate some religious moral code handed down to me by my grandparents or society. I had violated my own moral code. I was the villain. I was a terminally ill patient with no means for a cure. There was no reason for me to try and have a good life as life was just going to keep screwing me over like it had been. I told God I was tired of being beaten up, and I didn't need religion to give the final knockout punch. I got it already—I am awful.

A friend read Matthew 11:28 and Mark 2:17 to me. I gave my life to Jesus. As the old timers say I was saved that day. I have fallen and failed repeatedly, but I continually fall into the arms of Jesus. This is not a Jesus who demands nothing of me. This is not a Jesus of my own creation but Jesus who demands all of me, who loves me too much to leave me alone to my own device. I don't follow a Jesus that I create but the Jesus that in whom I am a new creation.

In my subjective truth experience when I have had times of deconstruction and doubt, I can come back to this time as a marker of something I experienced as a paradigm in my life. My life changed on that day. My perception of what could be possible and what was my true identity was forever shifted. We can make all the intellectual arguments for God we can (and we should), but the most powerful evidence there will ever be for God is a changed life. That day was not so much an event as a beginning of a relationship. Jesus, like the Little Prince and his Rose in the children's book written by Antoine de Saint-Exupéry, was taking time to transform and tame me. Jesus was taking responsibility for me like the Little Prince did for his rose. Jesus had made me his for all of eternity. Jesus likewise says of me and of you, "To be sure, an ordinary passerby would think that Jason looked just like any other human—Jason that belongs to me. But in himself alone he is more important than all the hundreds of other humans: because it is he that I have watered; because it is Jason that I have put under the glass globe; because it is Jason that I have sheltered behind the screen; because it is for Jason that I have killed the caterpillars (except the two or three that we saved to become butterflies); because it is Jason that I have listened to, when he grumbled, or boasted, or even sometimes when Jason said nothing. Because He is my rose." The only difference between The Little Prince's love for his rose and Jesus' love is that to Jesus every one of us is his rose. Friends, all we have to do is let Jesus be our Little Prince.

Father, when I was at the end of myself, wearied by my failures, tired of feeling alone, you were there. You left the ninety-nine roses for your rose. Even though I can grumbled or boast, or even sometimes ignore and neglect you, you still offer me rest simply because I am yours. I was sick, (most days I still am), and I need your healing work. I need your grace. I need you Jesus. Thank you. I can never thank you enough. I can't know your word or sing your praise enough to show you the gratitude you deserve. I love you Jesus. Amen.

38

The Glue and the Gold

And this is the testimony: God has given us eternal life, and this life is in his Son.

~1 John 5:11 NIV

On hearing this, Jesus said to them, "It is not the healthy who need a doctor, but the sick. I have not come to call the righteous, but sinners."

~Mark 2:17 NIV

"Amazing grace how sweet the sound, that saved a wretch like me. I once was lost, but now I'm found; was blind but now I see."

~John Newton

"Let us never forget that such a truth as this cannot be learned by rote as one would learn the facts of physical science. They must be experienced before we can really know them."

~A.W. Tozer

Kintsugi is a traditional Japanese technique of repairing

ceramics with lacquer and a metal powder, typically made from gold or silver. Meaning "joining with gold," this centuries-old practice is used to mend treasured objects, making their cracks beautiful and serving as a visual record of the object's history. In other words, kintsugi takes the cracked and broken pieces of a ceramic and draws attention to the imperfections by mending them with rice glue and gold. Kintsugi makes the brokenness the most beautiful part of the piece.

According to Merriam-Webster, a testimony is "a solemn declaration usually made by a witness under oath in response to interrogation by a lawyer or authorized public official; firsthand authentication of a fact; an outward sign; a public profession of a religious experience." What is a testimony if not a parable of God's kintsugi of a soul? A testimony is a recounting of how God's gift of eternal life through his son Jesus beautifies the cracks and broken fragments of a life. John Newton's powerful words articulate a testimony in song of the kintsugi-like work of the Holy Spirit. Our boast is the amazing grace of God in Christ Jesus.

At the end of the day people can debate, doubt, deconstruct, and dismiss fine intellectual arguments for and about cosmology, particularism, metaphysics, epistemology, the problem of evil. However, it is much harder to dismiss a testimony of a broken sinner who was once lost and is now found. How can someone refute a terminally ill man walking, skipping, jumping around long after his predicted death date? Every testimony shouts, *I was sick, and Jesus healed me. Jesus put me back together more beautifully than I thought imaginable even with all my scars, cracks, and brokenness.*

Friends, the redeeming work of Jesus is the glue and the gold that makes a broken life surrendered to the cross more beautiful than it could ever be without having been broken in the first place.

Father, thank you for putting me back together. Thank you that I was lost is a statement of the past and not one of my future. Holy Spirit, thank you for your continued redeeming work. Help me

137

Lord, to tell my story to all who will hear. Let me be confident that you can use even my testimony to further your kingdom. Lord, may you always be the glue and gold of my broken pieces. All glory and praise to Jesus. Amen.

39

Be kind and tender to one another. Forgive one another, just as God forgave you because of what Christ has done.
~Ephesians 4:32 NIVR

What should we say then? Since God is on our side, who can be against us?
~Romans 8:31 NIVR

"The story goes that a public sinner was excommunicated and forbidden entry to the church. He took his woes to God. 'They won't let me in, Lord, because I am a sinner. 'What are you complaining about?' said God. 'They won't let Me in either.'"
~Brennan Manning

"The greatest single cause of atheism in the world today is Christians who acknowledge Jesus with their lips and walk out the door and deny Him by their lifestyle. That is what an unbelieving world simply finds unbelievable.
~Brennan Manning

The time in my life when I doubted my beliefs the most by far and had the biggest deconstruction (near demolition) of my faith was, I was unfairly and unjustly kicked out of a Bible study. Essentially, I was disfellowshipped and rejected by my spiritual community. I spent an entire year without any fellowship with other Christians. I was secluded, hurt, and bitter. I doubted not so much God's existence at this time, but I did doubt God's goodness, and I completely deconstructed from thinking God had anything to do with church or Christians. I did have some Christians reach out during this time, but for about a year I became like a beat dog being offered a friendly hand. I did not trust that I would not be beat down more. My faith was damaged. It was not just doubt ,but my openness to the world of faith closed.

One of the only things that did not keep it from closing all together was that I was introduced to *The Ragamuffin Gospel* from Brennan Manning. It is not an exaggeration to say that Brennan Manning's work over the years has been medicine to my soul. This alcoholic Franciscan priest spoke to my heart. Brennan spoke of Jesus and reassured me that Jesus was madly and completely in love with me. He did not and would not reject me… ever… for any reason. Jesus was more disappointed with the actions of those in the Bible study than I was. Jesus rejected my excommunication. In a time where I had no friends, no fellowship, Jesus became my friend. I encountered a Jesus who was always on my side, not a Jesus of my own creation but the Jesus who always really was, and is, and is to come. As I began to see Jesus for who he really was I also began to see myself as the ragamuffin I truly was, broken, bedraggled, and dragged down by my own pride and selfishness.

Slowly I began to see the other people in the Bible study group the same way. After a while I read this quote—"Christians who acknowledge Jesus with their lips and walk out the door and deny Him by their lifestyle"—not as *those people*, but as me. Who was I to accept Jesus' forgiveness and not forgive myself? What gave me the right to be bitter when I had done so much wrong myself? What gave me the right to play the victim? They were victims too. We are all victims of being human. They were flawed, and frail ragamuffins like me. Once I could see them that way, which is who they always were, and not as the mentors I expected them to be, I began to forgive them.

While I was learning to love myself as Jesus did and love others, at the same time God was leading some of the people in the Bible study toward restoration and forgiveness. There is power in the words *I am sorry* if you aren't too bitter to let them sink in. Sorry does not deny the pain or perception and the experience of what happened, but it can dramatically reframe your perspective and experiences in the future. This event was incredibly painful and almost fully and permanently deconstructed my faith out of church, but healing did occur. Most of the relationships between myself and those in the Bible study were completely restored and ended up deeper and stronger than before. For that to happen, though, I had to do two things:

1. See myself as the wholly accepted completely loved child of God and friend to Jesus that I was/am, and
2. Understand that the enemy was not those people but a broken world and myself even if I was innocent in this particular situation.

Friends, once I grasped these two truths there was room for God to do his healing restorative work.

Father, help me to be kind and tender with other Christians. Lord, help me to be kind and tender with myself. Lord, grant me a heart that is as forgiving as yours is because of what Jesus did on the cross for sinners. Lord, help me to have confidence in your ability to heal and restore my soul. Lord help me to trust you to heal and restore broken relationships. Lord, thank you that I may walk in the confidence that you are for me. I am yours and nothing can change that. In the name of Jesus. Amen!

40

Surrender: Being the Villain in Your Own Story

So, obey God. Stand up to the devil. He will run away from you. Come near to God, and he will come near to you. Wash your hands, you sinners. Make your hearts pure, you who can't make up your minds. Be full of sorrow. Cry and weep. Change your laughter to mourning. Change your joy to sadness. Be humble in front of the Lord. And he will lift you up.

~James 4:7 NIVR

Lord, I know that people's lives are not their own; it is not for them to direct their steps.

~Jeremiah 10:23 NIV

"Come to me, all you who are tired and are carrying heavy loads. I will give you rest.

~Matthew 11:28 NIV

"We must not wish for the disappearance of our troubles but for the grace to transform them."

~Simone Weil

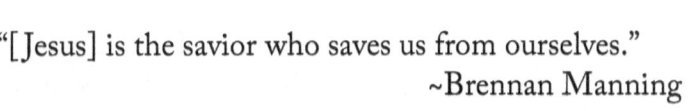

"[Jesus] is the savior who saves us from ourselves."
~Brennan Manning

I had just cut a very frustrating day in the recording studio short and was just about to sit down on the couch for a snack when my wife (at the time) walked in the house with a manila envelope in hand and her father behind her. It was a shock as she was supposed to be at work and her dad lived two states away, but I immediately knew what it meant. I had no clue our problems were that serious five minutes before, but when I saw that entrance, I knew what was in that envelope. She was divorcing me.

She asked me in the bedroom and told me that she wasn't happy and had not been in a long time. She asserted that I was not happy either. She was right on both accounts. I protested that I knew we were in a slump, but I thought we would pull through it. She told me she did not want to pull through it, but she knew I would want to see the kids so thought it best we work through this amicably. I told her I did not understand. What happened that was so bad that we could not get through it? She said she didn't want to talk about it now. I asked her to write it down, all of it, in a letter so I would know. I asked her to do this and to give me a chance. She agreed to the letter but not the chance.

Although I was a Christian (and a for-real one) I had been a selfish, self-absorbed, neglectful, temperamental, and often border-line emotionally abusive husband. I had not put her needs above my own. I had not treated her the way Christ treats his church. This situation was self-inflicted. I was the villain. I was the villain, and I could not fix it. I am the reason the marriage failed. Over the next year I read every book I could on marriage and becoming the kind of man she could love. I came off the road, quit my band, gave up my record deal, and began to work in the corporate world. I went to divorce care; I went to counseling. I was accountable to other men.

But ultimately the divorce went through. I had done the work, but it was too little too late. Despite this being the worst six months of my life—I lost my marriage, my career, and my dad to cancer all in a very short period of time—I was finally ready to be used by God, because I was ready to be saved from myself. I was done with my plans, my agenda, my preoccupations, and my pride.

Friends, it wasn't until I became utterly done with myself; it was not until I realized how eternally useless my intellect or talent is without God that I was ready to be used by him. Over the next few years in a very Job like manner, my children and I got closer than ever, I got my music career back, and I met my now wife. I learned by coming to the end of myself that God not only loves me but likes me when I get out of his way to do so.

Lord, humble me in all the ways I have yet to be humbled. Clean out the diseases of selfishness and pride that I don't even know or would be brave enough to admit are there deep in my heart. Holy Spirit, lay heavy on my heart my sin, so I can surrender it to you for you to do your healing, redemptive, and restorative work. Lord, I give you my life, I dare not take it as my own. Lord, I don't ask that you remove my troubles only that you strengthen me and change me through them. When I get weary and beat down by my troubles, let me go nowhere but to you, Jesus, who are familiar with my troubles and will take the burden for me. In the name of Jesus. Amen.

41

Spiritual Post-Op

When he saw the crowds, he had compassion for them, because they were harassed and helpless, like sheep without a shepherd
~Matthew 9:36 NIVR

For what I received I passed on to you as of first importance that Christ died for our sins according to the Scriptures, that he was buried, that he was raised on the third day according to the Scriptures.
~1 Corinthians 15:3–4 NIV

God was bringing the world back to himself through Christ. He did not hold people's sins against them. God has trusted us with the message that people may be brought back to him.
~2 Corinthians 5:19 NIVR

At just the right time Christ died for ungodly people. He died for us when we had no power of our own. It is unusual for anyone to die for a godly person. Maybe someone would be willing to die for a good person. But here is how God has shown his love for us. While we were still sinners, Christ died for us.
~Romans 5:6–8 NIVR

Say with your mouth, "Jesus is Lord." Believe in your heart that God raised him from the dead. Then you will be saved. With your heart you believe and are made right with God. With your mouth you say what you believe. And so, you are saved.
~Romans 10:9–10 NIVR

"The gospel is absurd, and the life of Jesus is meaningless unless we believe that He lived, died, and rose again with but one purpose in mind: to make brand-new creations. Not to make people with better morals but to create a community of prophets and professional lovers, men and women who would surrender to the mystery of the fire of the Spirit that burns within, who would live in ever greater fidelity to the omnipresent Word of God, who would enter into the center of it all, the very heart and mystery of Christ, into the center of the flame that consumes, purifies, and sets everything aglow with peace, joy, boldness, and extravagant, furious love. This, my friend, is what it really means to be a Christian."

~Brennan Manning

"Sin is not a legal problem because God is not a lawyer. Sin is a death problem. It's far more like a disease than anything else."

~Fr. Stephen Freeman

In Jesus, God came near. Near to the brokenhearted, near to the disaffected; close to those who feel they suffer alone; he has compassion on those who doubt; he understands those who question; he is not offended by those who deconstruct; even when one walks away, he longs for them to let him come near again; he loves those who don't feel loved and accepts those who don't feel accepted. He is the God of the outcast and the downtrodden. He is the God who has compassion on the broken. He only wants to put us back together again and make us more beautiful. What the free choices of free humans had broken, Jesus came to reconcile. We have all broken our own standard of morality by our own free choices, so how much more have we each broken God's heart by our free choices?

My salvation, my testimony is my restoration story. My story of being spiritually healed. My life is in post-op. The surgery is complete and the terminal disease removed. I have a new identity for the rest of time. My identity is spiritual death survivor (Romans 6:23; Ephesians 2:1; Colossians 2:13). The rest of my life is recovery. The rest of my life is spiritual therapy, teaching my soul to live and function in the reality of being free from disease. The terminal disease of spiritual death is terminally gone. I am cured, spiritual death isn't in permanent remission, it is eradicated. I was cured by the surgeon's love, his careful hand, his wisdom and ultimately his sacrifice. See in this surgery the surgeon himself had to not just remove the disease from me but had to take it on himself. Now nothing can separate me from the surgeon who himself is the cure. I am convinced that nothing in all creation, will be able to separate us from the love of the surgeon that is Christ Jesus our Lord. The symptoms of spiritual death (pride, greed, lust, envy, gluttony, wrath, laziness) may still linger in presentation, but the symptoms are phantom. Any spiritual limps, aches or pains I have now are the bodily muscle memory of the flesh that has not yet learned the reality. I don't need to walk with a limp anymore. If I follow doctor's orders the lingering phantom symptoms will get smaller and less noticeable over time. The more I exercise and remain disciplined in the spiritual therapy I have been prescribed, the less obvious the presentation of the phantom symptoms will be.

The great physician has performed a successful surgery, my identity has changed from a person riddled with disease to one who is disease free. I just must learn to live in the reality of that. The soul is fully healed even if the flesh (the body; the senses, the brain) doesn't know it and isn't fully capable of living it yet.

Salvation in Christ is not primarily a legal matter. It is not just about transferring a name from the guilty side of the ledger to the innocent side of the ledger (though that is very much the case). Jesus is far more the great physician than the great lawyer. Friends, God will for sure act as judge, but his primary role and desire is that of healer.

The great physician, Lord thank you for coming near to me for me. Even before I knew I needed you, you came near. I thank you for taking on and curing the disease of sin. The disease that those who came before me chose for me and that I chose by my own free will. Thank you for your sacrifice on the cross, thank you for the new life of the resurrection and thank you for loving me before and more than I could love you or myself. Lord, I repent for choosing myself and my ways over you. I am self-interested and self-destructive far too often and yet you have compassion on me. You do not hold my sins against me. Jesus is Lord! Jesus is Lord! I am a new creation in Jesus! Jesus is Lord. Amen.

42

The Words of Life:
The Holy One of God

From this time many of his disciples turned back and no longer followed him. 'You do not want to leave too, do you?' Jesus asked the Twelve. Simon Peter answered him, 'Lord, to whom shall we go? You have the words of eternal life. We have come to believe and to know that you are the Holy One of God.
~John 6:66–69 NIV

"Christianity is not simply a message but an experience of faith that becomes a message."

~Brennan Manning

"It is really true what philosophy tells us, that life must be understood backwards. But with this, one forgets the second proposition, that it must be lived forwards. A proposition which, the more it is subjected to careful thought, the more it ends up concluding precisely that life at any given moment cannot really ever be fully understood; exactly because there is no single moment where time stops completely in order for me to take position [to do this]: going backwards."

~Soren Kierkegaard

149

Often our intellectual doubts and deconstructions are birthed from painful personal experience. Likewise, our faith and reconstructions are birthed from positive personal experiences. As we live and gain more and more understanding of our experiences, our perception can change. We can even come to see the redemptive nature of our most painful experiences even if we never fully understand why we had to go through them. The redemptive transformation of all of our experiences is the core message of Christianity.

In my experience most of the time when I grow in faith it is on the backside of a period of doubt. When I have perceived a mountain elation in God's presence it is almost always after a time of pain and disappointment. All humans will have doubts about their belief system and worldview. All humans live by putting their faith in their belief system and worldview. I have deconstructed and reconstructed many of my beliefs. I doubt easy and believe hard. I don't have any delusions that I am done with doubt. I fully expect that I will deconstruct several of my beliefs and have to reconstruct them again. I fully expect I'll doubt again, and you should to. It is okay, doubt is an integral part of faith. It is certainty that is faith's enemy.

I think it is important that we put the critical eye on what is causing our doubts as much as the doubting of beliefs we once held firm. I have found that if I give my faith a fair shake it can stand up against and hold its own with any counter view. Friends, I have always been able to reconstruct my faith with more intellectual and experiential integrity than I have in leaving it. I am beginning to doubt that will ever change. Where else am I going to go? I know that Jesus has the words of life, and I continue to come back to the belief that Jesus is the Holy One of God.

My friend and brother Jesus. My savior and Lord. Jesus, be the delight and pleasure of my often-wandering soul. You are my reassurance in doubts. Help me to doubt my doubt even more than I doubt my beliefs. You are the Lord of my deconstructions and reconstructions. You are the redeemer of my painful experiences, the one I can return to over and over even in despair. You are my light and guide in every uncertainty and confusion, you are the forgiver of my failures, the securer of my faith and salvation, my rock when my thoughts are sinking in sand. Lord, you still love me even when what you say is right doesn't seem right to me. You are patient with my questions and questioning. Help me by gifting me the wisdom in these times to understand why you say what you say but the wisdom to trust you even when I can't understand.

Jesus, you are the one who is so very longsuffering with me when I am trying to work things out, even when it is taking far longer than it should. Jesus, you have proven yourself over and over again, you are the one that I can always trust, even when I can't figure out who to trust. You have the words to life and are the Holy One of God. Jesus, build my faith in these truths, in your Holy faithful name. Amen.

About the Author

Dr. Jason Lee McKinney is a professor, internationally touring singer, multiple award-winning songwriter and recording artist, and lay philosopher. Dr. McKinney holds a BA in Management, an MBA, an MA in Philosophy and Apologetics, and an Ed.D in Leadership and Professional Practice. Dr. McKinney resides in Nashville with his wife Summer (a therapist and author) and eight-year old son Kai (a drum phenom). The McKinneys also have two grown sons—Zeke (a recording artist for Tooth & Nail records) and Zion (a worship leader at LifePoint church), one grown daughter, Zakyra (who is studying to be a theater teacher) and one daughter-in-law, Juliana (a middle school choir director and wife to Zion).

also available from

WordCrafts Press

Aerobics for the Mind
Michael Potts, PhD

I Wish Someone Had Told Me
Barbie Loflin

A Pastor's Secrets
Ronnie Meek

I AM
Summer McKinney

www.wordcrafts.net

www.ingramcontent.com/pod-product-compliance
Lightning Source LLC
Chambersburg PA
CBHW031530120626
46545CB00005B/2077